Crowd Culture

BERNARD IDDINGS BELL

Crowd Culture

An Examination of
the American Way of Life

Introduction by
CICERO BRUCE

ISI Books
Wilmington, Delaware
2001

488 58120

Cataloging-in-Publication Data

Bell, Bernard Iddings, 1886-1958.
   Crowd culture : an examination of the American way of life / by Bernard Iddings Bell ; new introduction by Cicero Bruce. —4th ed. — Wilmington, DE : ISI Books, 2001.
      p. ; cm.

"The following chapters were lectures delivered on April 22, 1952, at Ohio Wesleyan University, on the Frederick Merrick Foundation." —Foreword. Includes index.

   ISBN 1-882926-60-9
         1. United States—Civilization—1945- 2. Education—United States. 3. United States—Religion—1945-1960. 4. United States—Religion—1960- I. Title.

E169.2 .B36 2001   01-110952
973.9—dc21   CIP

Published in the United States by:
ISI Books
Post Office Box 4431
Wilmington, DE 19807-0431

Manufactured in the United States of America

Contents

Introduction

IF THE TWENTIETH CENTURY WAS A STREAM RUSHING madly toward a maelstrom, Bernard Iddings Bell, a champion of orthodoxy, swam defiantly against the flow. What he withstood was the violent current of modernity that threatens to crush any non-utilitarian concept of life—the humane traditions that support civilization. He embraced Christianity and believed that, because God created them, men and women are fundamentally religious beings whose real world exists in a common creaturehood of the spirit. He opposed revelation to naturalism, faith to doubt, authority to personality, wisdom to mere knowledge. He was no intellectual trimmer, no moral eclectic, and certainly no fashionable nihilist. He was a staunch conservator who called his contemporaries back to what is vital to the human condition.

Bell made this call most deliberately in some twenty controversial books in which he rigorously examined the cultural manifestations of the muddled modern mind. Among his principal works are *Right and Wrong After the War* (1918), *Postmodernism and Other Essays* (1926), *Beyond Agnosticism* (1929), *Unfashionable Convictions* (1931), *In the City of Confusion* (1938), *The Church in Disrepute*

(1943), *God Is Not Dead* (1945), and *Crisis in Education* (1949). These insightful little books attracted considerable attention when they were published, many of them beginning as articles in the *New York Times Magazine, Commonweal,* and the *Atlantic Monthly.*

By 1950, Bell, an ordained priest in the Episcopal church, was known as one of the most distinguished Christian writers in America, and he was admired by some of the more formidable conservatives of the time, men such as Albert J. Nock, T. S. Eliot, and Richard M. Weaver. Writing before the rise of academic specialization, few theologians have reached as wide and diverse a public as Bell did during the first half of the last century. His audience extended to England and Canada, where he frequently toured and read from his works. His books deeply influenced a number of prominent men and women of letters, including a young Russell Kirk who placed Bell in the "literary party of order," that faction of writers past, present, and to come for whom the order of the soul is paramount.

Like Kirk, Bell was ashamed of the last century and its patrimonial squandering. Yet, to be ashamed of having been born into the twentieth century was—for both men—to be, in some sense at least, a decent human being in an age of indecency. As Kirk tells us in his memoir *The Sword of Imagination,* Bell was a prophet for the age, "an Isaiah preaching to the Remnant," a High Churchman who conceded nothing "to the social gospellers, liberals, latitudinarians, modernists, humanitarians, or public-relations experts." Bell, writes Kirk—who praised but few as unreservedly as he did his hierophantic friend—was "so hot against entrenched selfishness and stupidity" that he was once accused of being a communist. He was so averse to collectivism that he was "denounced as an apologist for reaction." Such derision, Kirk hastens to add, delighted Bell, who rejoiced in an intellectual skirmish. "No one...ever had the better of him in a battle of wits." Although quick to fight, Bell was always ready to forgive, and to be forgiven. He was, in Kirk's words, "a man of honor—jealous of his own honor, scrupulous in distinguishing persons from opinions."

Born on 13 October 1886, in Dayton, Ohio, Bell was the son of Charles Wright and Vienna Valencia (Iddings) Bell. He received a B.A. in 1907 from the University of Chicago, where he majored in social history, took part in plays, wrote for sundry college publications, and survived a severe bout of skepticism by reading G. K. Chesterton's *Orthodoxy*. He studied religion at Western Theological Seminary (which later became Seabury Western Seminary), where he graduated in 1912 with a bachelor's degree in sacred theology. In 1919, after serving as vicar and dean of St. Paul's Church in Fond du

Lac, Wisconsin, he accepted an offer to preside as warden at St. Stephen's College (now Bard College) in New York, a position he held until 1933. While at St. Stephen's he taught religion at Columbia University. As canon of St. John's Cathedral in Rhode Island, as canon of the Cathedral of Saints Peter and Paul in Illinois, and as William Vaughn Moody Lecturer at the University of Chicago, Bell dedicated his later years to the religious training of adults and to teaching in the classroom. In 1958 he left this life for the next, bequeathing precious little by which to remember him but the books through which he tried to reach an age which he knew was getting and spending itself to death.

Until now, all of these books were out of print. Like so many sapient voices of the last century, Bell's has been dinned out of hearing by what W. B. Yeats called "the noisy set...the martyrs call the world." The reign of error in academia and publishers in the clutch of a secularist ideology have muted the minority voice whose point of view challenges the current melioristic *Weltanschauung*. This suppression is lamentable as it further reveals the liberal bias so prevalent in American culture. Few who now profess the humanities have heard the name Bernard Iddings Bell. But most, alas, are quite familiar with John Dewey, whose radical democratization of education Bell courageously excoriated. Given academe's hegemonic dominion over the presses and popular opinion, it should surprise no one that, while over thirty works by Professor Dewey remain in print, Bell's books have long been unpurchasable.

To be sure, Bell's books can be found scattered upon the dustier shelves of many good libraries across the country. However, they ought to be for sale in America's best bookstores. Many of them are as pertinent today as when they were written, and if the coming decades are as spiritually dry and philosophically disoriented as the last half of the twentieth century, these books will retain their relevance. In each, Bell tempers his independence of thought with the wisdom of the human race and proceeds with faith, hope, and charity—as a believing Christian who loves human beings and refuses to despair. Nor does he ignore the latest discoveries of science or fail to consider modern philosophy and popular psychology. Nonetheless, he does not write as a modernist, for the modernist offers no remedy to the moral problems that plague contemporary man. Rather, Bell writes as a diagnostician of the moral commonwealth, as a critic with the courage to judge.

Of all his books, *Crowd Culture,* reprinted here for the first time in over thirty years, stands as Bell's greatest achievement. *Crowd Culture* is a feat of Chestertonian strength, written for the everlasting man. Moreover, it is Bell's most essential work. Here in four limpid chapters, published originally six years before his death, is a condensation of his thought on the culture of consumption, the slums of mass education, the misguided modernization of the church, and the intelligent but humble resistance of the few. "What Bell has said in this book," wrote Eliot in a review, "he will say, I hope, again and again; and if he says it often enough, and if people begin saying the same things, there may be some changes for the better in 25 or 50 years." With the present reprint, Bell speaks out yet again. He speaks to the thoughtful of the current generation, just as he spoke to three preceding generations of thinking men and women.

Bell minces no words in this apt commentary on the American way of life. In "The Cultural Picture," he notes that "ours is a nation of new-rich people, well-washed, all dressed up, rather pathetically unsure just what it is dressed up for; a nation convinced that a multitude of material goods, standardized, furiously and expensively advertised by appeals to greed and vanity, will in themselves make life worth the living." Obviously, Bell believed that Americans are, in general, crass and crude. They are crass and crude not because they want intelligence or technological ingenuity; they are undeniably clever and scientifically more advanced than any other people. No, they are crass and crude because they no longer interest themselves in eternal questions and ultimate concerns.

Being unused to money and therefore easily deceived by its glitter, Americans, of the kind Bell depicts in *Crowd Culture,* too often confuse happiness with purchasable commodities, and fail to realize that genuine happiness transcends the realm of advertisement. What the old-rich know about money, Bell observes, the new-rich realize, if at all, only after they have grown accustomed to their earthly possessions. Those who never accustom themselves sacrifice their lives, and even their children, to the gods of the world and of the flesh.

Implicated in what Bell considers the world are not the wonders of nature, not the creative labors of pious men and women, not the pursuit of sapience with which to live humanely, but the "nonsense of supposing that externalities possessed ennoble the owners, that a full fist invariably indicates a fine spirit." The object of the average man of the world—of the crowd—is neither justice nor liberty; it is, on the contrary, money and recognition. Bell reminds us that the defining characteristic of any culture is its *cult*—its religion—and the predominant cult in America is none other than the world of personality. What Americans erect as their object of perpetual adoration is the man or woman with money, the mundane movie star, the overpaid professional athlete.

Americans believe, and teach their children to believe, that the wealthiest of the crowd are good and virtuous, and that the child who is good and virtuous will be wealthy by that very fact. Anyone, Bell objects, who knows the true meaning of goodness and virtue surely recognizes the error of this belief. Every sage of moral vision has warned that greedily amassed fortunes tend to isolate their owners, to render them vulnerable, a bit trifling if not a little ludicrous. One who takes time to study the lives of the truly great figures who have risen above the world knows that wealth is rarely the reward for pursuing the good and the virtuous. Bell himself committed his life to serving others and defending seemingly lost causes only to die blind and poor.

In sacrificing himself to the gods of the flesh, the average American worships comfort. He sets up comfort as the *summum bonum,* and he does so because he proceeds from the premise that man must surmount all suffering to fulfill his destiny. This premise is false, as Bell asserts time and again in the succeeding chapters, because it is based on the positivistic belief that, if man could only perfect his environment and eliminate all human suffering, he could, in the process, remake himself. Such is the operative premise of the mechanist who, according to Bell, refuses to accept that one must of necessity struggle to become and remain human. The mechanistic view contradicts the Christian understanding of human nature based on the doctrine of original sin. Moreover, it denies the reality of the human soul, which is, in truth, tested and forged by quotidian trials and perturbations. While Americans of true character recognize the absurdity of the mechanistic premise, "all too few," writes Bell, "ask whether it can possibly be that, since our primeval ancestors crawled from the slime of the sea, first the animal world and then the human race have struggled on, at cost of travail and pain and tears and death, merely that modern man may sit down and be comfortable."

Most Americans rarely ask such questions because they resemble the "vertical intruder" that Ortega y Gasset envisages in *The Revolt of the Masses,* an illuminating commentary which Bell lauded as one of those books that one must read to understand the cultural development of modern times. The crowd-loving American, like Ortega's vertical intruder, has invaded civilization from the basement and taken possession of the drawing room. "This is to the good," Bell admits, "but possession of the drawing room is not of great value, is often embarrassing, to the Common Man, unless he has learned how to use the drawing room, unless he knows the amenities." The schools and the churches, those institutions which Bell deems most capable of showing America's vertical intruder how to behave in civilization's upper rooms, have so far failed to train those who might otherwise prevent what may ultimately be the uncivil destruction of the whole house.

That the schools were failing America was painfully clear to a handful of thinkers who expressed concern early in the last century. In 1908, Irving Babbitt underscored the root causes of this failing in his prescient book *Literature and the American College*. Seven years later, in *Aristocracy and Justice*, Paul Elmer More wrote: "We must get back to a common understanding of the office of education in the construction of society and must discriminate among the subjects that may enter into the curriculum by their relative value towards this end."

Skeptical though they were, Babbitt and More at least considered education redeemable. By 1930, however, Bell and others in the literary party of order were convinced that the schools had lost any common assumptions as to the aim of education. To them the universities in particular appeared to be in such a state of anomie that nothing short of divine intervention could save them from disaster. One might hope, said Eliot in his 1933 address to the Classical Club of Harvard, that America's universities would eventually learn to follow what is timeless, time-tested, and time-honored, "or be relegated to preservation as curious architectural remains; but they cannot be expected to lead." At the modern university it is virtually impossible for a young soul to get a genuine "critical, literary education," remarked Allen Tate in a 1940 essay. The student of mass education is unable to discuss a work of literature "in terms of its specific form; all he can do is to give you its history or tell you how he *feels* about it." If one goes to graduate school, declared Tate, "he comes out incapacitated for criticism; if he tries to be a critic he is not unlike the ignorant impressionist who did not go to graduate school."

Having been an elementary school teacher, a high school teacher, and a college professor and president, Bell was well acquainted with the failings of modern education. What is more, he was determined to expose the party responsible for these failings, the party of John Dewey. Schools predicated upon "Dewey's philosophy or any other relativistic philosophy are," as Bell put it, "only too likely to produce alumni who have no definite standards of right and wrong, who judge words and deeds only by whether they seem expedient in a given, temporary, set of circumstances."

If such alumni seem to be the norm today, they are so because the academics who taught them are, as Bell reminds us, Dewey's apostles and, in their apostolic succession, the bane of education. Deweyism was—and still is—

a formidable force. Yet Bell stood boldly against its degrading tendencies, and with the first publication of *Crowd Culture* he found many allies. Russell Kirk hoped and prayed that these allies might well-nigh "cleanse the intellectual sty in the closing years of the twentieth century." But they did not. The job remains to be done. Today, America needs dozens more reformers of Bell's ilk to lead it out of the same, if superficially altered, crisis in education with which Bell deals in "The School."

In this chapter Bell reveals what he believes to be an undeniable correlation between the manner in which Americans are illiberally educated and their apparent inability to conduct themselves as gentle men and women. He observes that what traditionally distinguished the gentle man and woman from their common counterparts was not that the former possessed more worldly goods than the latter (for often the gentle man and woman were anything but wealthy). What distinguished the former from the latter was that the gentle man and woman had, while the common man and woman lacked, a principled education informed by what Chateaubriand called the genius of Christianity, an education which had as its end the realization of a unifying vision of nature and man's place in it. Granted, the gentle man and woman, the natural leaders of the people, did not always govern justly. But having studied civilization and the moral precepts that make it possible, they at least governed intelligently.

Although Bell affirms the right of the common man and woman to govern themselves, he insists that they can do so responsibly, and with dignity, only if they are humanely educated. Here, he quotes Thomas Jefferson: "I know no safe depository of the ultimate powers of society but the people themselves; and if we think them not enlightened enough to exercise control with a wholesome discretion, the remedy is not to take it from them but to inform their discretion by education." For Bell, informing the discretion of the people entails, first and foremost, instructing them in the ways of virtue. The people must be led to understand "that both the making of their souls and also their most real service to our country depend upon their finding deliverance for themselves from the pursuit of such obvious and ostentatious trivialities as satisfy the masses at the moment." Moreover, informing their discretion requires that those who do the instructing remember that the proper study of mankind is man—nothing more, and certainly nothing less.

It is, at bottom, this fact that the modern academic has forgotten, particularly at the university where, according to Bell, one finds an increasing number of tenured neoterists bent on subverting what was once viewed as the true and the good. While he respected meaningful scholarship, supported and involved himself in the perennial pursuit of knowledge, Bell felt that in many ways academe was fast becoming an asylum for half-educated intellectuals who, having cut themselves loose from all religious moorings, pursued erudition only as a means to avoid the Absolute. He knew that many university professors are committed nominalists who believe, and would have everybody else believe, that universals such as truth, justice, and salvation exist in name only, as nothing more than human desiderata; that reality exists in the subjective mind alone; that there are as many universes as there are minds thinking them into existence; that the transcendent and organizing center of language cannot hold because there never was a transcendent center in the first place; that in the beginning there was *nada*, and *nada* was with *nada*, and *nada* was *nada*.

Because he thought that any activity related to education, whether pedagogical or scholarly in kind, ought to be completed from a definite moral point of view, Bell naturally abhorred the intransigent postmodern tenet that all views are relative. He discerned correctly that the teacher who holds such an erroneous opinion has grown bored with the proper study of mankind. And, moreover, students under the tutelage of such a one are certain to confuse right with wrong, virtue with vice, good with evil, authority with force, having no fixed axioms by which to orient themselves in the flux.

The academics whom Bell indicts have replaced the study of man with the study of progress. Although they deny the existence of absolutes, they paradoxically subscribe *absolutely* to the notion that the man of today is a fundamentally different creature from the man of five hundred years ago. All that they teach in the classroom derives from this assumption, an assumption that goes, more often than not, unchallenged. It would be one thing were the crowd alone enchanted by the idea of progress. That the supposedly educated and wiser members of society promote progress as an incontrovertible principle by which to live is quite another. Its establishment as such proves once again that what begins in the ivory towers of higher learning soon becomes accepted as truth in the thoroughfares of America. Moreover, the unexamined acceptance of progress as a truism to be acknowledged by all belies the hope that falsehood will be exposed in the proverbial marketplace of ideas. Of all the suppositions peddled as absolute truth, the myth of progress, Bell contends, is by far one of the most insidious.

Until the myth of progress comes under scrutiny, the American student, Bell warns, will remain a provincial of contemporaneity, unable and disinclined to reform himself, much less society, in light of the perennial truths about the nature and destiny of mankind that have guided men through the centuries. Only when he sees man as he has been, says Bell, can the student begin to know man as he is. And he can see most vividly what man has been by immersing himself in the Western literary tradition. To teach the myth of progress and those attendant studies that reduce the pursuit of genuine liberal learning to narrowly focused discussions (on, say, race, class, and gender) instead of imparting the wisdom of the noble dead is, as Bell intimates throughout the middle chapters of this book, to rob the student of his intellectual inheritance, or as Paul Elmer More puts it, to debauch his "mind with a flabby, or inflame it with a frantic, humanitarianism."

In having truckled to humanitarianism, the churches, Bell argues, have become as ineffectual as the academy in providing America with the kind of citizens it sorely needs. Bell accuses contemporary churches of ceasing, on the whole, to perform "the primary task of confronting mundane cultures with external morality, confronting a failing world with God." In their misguided attempts to be "up-to-date," he says, churches of all denominations have gradually conformed themselves to the ways of unregenerate man. What the clergy have forgotten in their diffident acquiescence to the demands of popular culture is that God expects his church to be something more than a "promoter of a respectable minor art, charming if it happens to appeal to you, its only moral function to bless whatever the multitude at the moment regards as the American way of life." God intends his church to be nothing less than "His mystical Body, made up of those committed to the task of moral resistance to the world."

What many lay people really want to hear from the pulpit, as Bell knew from firsthand experience as a cleric, is not the tedious chant of progress, but instead the resounding note of faith in everlasting truths. What alienates those who seek the truly sacred is not that the churches are too religious, but that many of them are simply not religious enough. Those who look to the churches for spiritual answers to what ails their souls too often find that the so-called religious leaders have degenerated into what Bell describes as little private chaplains of the worldly, flattering and validating the irreverent lives of their patrons.

Carried along by the obstreperous currents of popular culture, the very Christians who pride themselves on their "contemporary worship services," are, Bell believed, complicit in the profanation of the sacred, in the estrangement of secularly educated adolescents, and in the erection of American institutions on pragmatic rather than permanent principles. Modern Christians of the kind Bell takes to task in *Crowd Culture* have become, most regrettably, "an uncommitted host of politely respectable people, willing to be led by professional ecclesiastics whose methods of promotion and administration are just about as worldly as those of the sick society they say they wish to reform but which, as a matter of fact, deforms them almost as easily as it deforms everybody else."

Bell also discerns a lack of courage and conviction on the part of those Christians who are directly and indirectly responsible for providing America's youth with religious instruction. Most negligent, he says, are the parents. Influenced by the sophists of modernity, many parents help to perpetuate the false belief that religious instruction is anything but a necessary part of a balanced education. That religious training ought to play an important role in education is to most parents an obscure proposition.

America is in serious trouble, Bell cautions. Its way of life resembles what Plato envisioned as the epitome of radical egalitarianism: the father condescending to his children lest they shun him; the mother affecting their frivolous manners from fear of being thought dull or authoritarian; the child impudently contradicting his parents; the schoolmaster flattering his pupils; and the pupils despising their teachers and tutors. America, Bell warns, is mired in a provincialism not of country or county—but of time and spirit. Its schools serve the vagaries of demos. Its educators, full of passionate intensity, circumscribe young, impressionable minds in an intellectually narrow presentism. Its churches make man the measure of all things and fail to redeem the fallen world by bringing the Eternal into the temporal. The religious seek to preserve themselves at the cost of unconscionable compromise. They are reluctant to speak the truth of God and man—nor do they appear sure just what that truth is. Their worship tends to be prosaic, their morality largely sentimental.

Faced with schools that reduce education to nothing other than job training, faced with churches singing alternative hymns instead of chanting creeds, faced with a pervasive and decadent popular culture—faced with all this, America, Bell maintains, is unlikely to recover its senses until a "democratic elite" rises up from the people to guide the crowd "into a more urbane and humane way of living." Avowing his hope that an elite of this kind would indeed emerge, he devoted the final chapter of *Crowd Culture* to an extensive description of the adversity such a group would have to overcome and the kind of education it would need in order to triumph.

Bell makes it clear that one who would join this band of rebels must first of all expect to be poor. He must also settle for scant recognition and little preferment for what he does, even when he works to improve institutions like universities and churches. Worst of all he must endure the scorn of his children, who may resent living in frugal contradistinction to their more fashionable neighbors. "Woe be to his wife," Bell writes, "if she be not devoted to the improvident ideals and purposes to the same degree as her husband." In brief, he who chooses to oppose the crowd must be willing to live as an ascetic, motivated by "much the same sort of impulse, and willingly embracing much the same sort of discipline, as are known to him who forsakes the secular world for the cloister." Unlike those who sequester themselves, however, he who chooses to guide the madding crowd must stand in its midst.

He must also receive as fine a liberal arts education as he possibly can. This end is not always achieved by way of formal schooling, says Bell. In fact, it is often hindered by organized, overly compartmentalized education. What is chiefly important is that the rebel keep in mind the object of learning. Although his education was at best rudimentary, Abraham Lincoln "taught himself," Bell points out, "and he made a good job of it largely because he knew the kind of understanding he was after and then with labor pursued the getting of it." Like Lincoln, he who would lead rather than follow the crowd must know the difference between genuine education and pseudo-education, between a good school and a bad one. Good schools can be a great boon; bad ones can do irreparable harm. This statement holds true at all levels of education.

Bell goes on to say that those who know the kind of

learning they need to lead the crowd will not covet academic degrees. "Academic degrees are not significant," he says, "unless one knows in what fields they were taken, in what spirit the study was directed, for what ends it was undertaken and brought to completion." Working assiduously to earn a Ph.D. is surely a commendable exercise in discipline. "But discipline alone within some narrow field," says Bell, in words which echo Irving Babbitt's in *Literature and the American College*, "does not insure competence for living." Only a basic study of what it means to be human can insure that.

Nor will the aspirant who knows the importance of humane learning content himself by specializing in one abstract science or another, Bell continues, valuable though the sciences are. One may excel in one's knowledge of, say, thermodynamics and still be morally ignorant. Information for information's sake will not in and of itself help anyone to conserve civilization. As Bell argues in the final pages of this thin but insightful book, one needs information *plus* some basic metaphysical first principles "if one is to become fit to help direct a culture intelligently or even oneself to participate in a culture." The rebel that Bell visualizes will learn the significance of such principles not from an intellectual flirtation with science and software, but from a disciplined study of created man, whom God endowed with a moral consciousness.

Such a study must of necessity include history, writes Bell, "the record not merely of man's economic and governmental arrangements and disarrangements but of man's groping attempts to find meaning, his striving to maintain self-respect, his endeavor to live with other men in mutual joy despite continual disillusionments, his frequent near despairs, his grounds for hope." History, as Bell defines it, is that study by which one comes to see in the past an enduring order and purpose teleologically defined by the Eternal. One studies "man's failures," Bell tells us, to gain "humility and compassion." One considers "man's occasional successes" to know "the price which must be paid to become and remain adequately a husband or a wife, a parent, a friend, a lover, a citizen, a human being." History, as Bell understands it and would have us understand it, is nothing less than the past realized in the present, the present realized in the past. It is not, as the New Historicists would make of it, a bolus upon which to impose an ideological methodology. It is, on the contrary, an integral relationship of parts to a whole through which, and in which, the Logos is made manifest.

The study of created man must go beyond pure history, however. To be complete, says Bell, this study must engage the philosophers. Furthermore, it should extend to the best of imaginative literature, particularly vatic poetry, which Richard Weaver called the "surest antidote to the vices of sentimentality and brutality." Moreover, the study of man *qua* man ought to entail a sincere examination of music, dance, sculpture, painting, and theater; from these strivings to achieve a significant creativeness one gains indispensable insights into the human predicament. And, yes, the study of man, rightly conceived, must take into account his religion, for man is by nature, and by divine plan, a religious being whose essential dignity depends finally upon his Maker.

In describing the formation of an elite to guide the crowd, Bell echoed other visionaries in the literary party of order. Babbitt, for one, called for an "aristocracy of character and intelligence...to take the place of an aristocracy of birth, and to counteract the tendency toward an aristocracy of money." In a letter to Paul Elmer More, Eliot expressed his hope that a "new type of intellectual" would come into being, one "combining the intellectual and the devotional." Neither the "purely intellectual Christian" nor the "purely emotional Christian" will suffice, Eliot said, to combat the humanitarianism of a spiritually regressive age like the present. This new kind of intellectual must, Eliot insisted, have "hold of the tip of the tail of something quite real, more real than morals or than sweetness and light and culture." This new being and his fellow aristocrats must, according to the literary party of order, be as medieval-minded as they are modern. They must stand in stark contrast to the squabbling demagogue who climbs to power on the backs of the crowd whom he flatters. They must lead, as More put it, "by imposing their authority and experience on the impulsive emotions of the multitude."

Since *Crowd Culture* first appeared in print, America has changed in many ways for the better. The civil rights movement, for example, certainly improved the moral integrity of the country. Yet in many more ways America has changed for the worse. The same decade that gave rise to the Civil Rights Act spawned a selfish individualism, which made possible *Roe v. Wade*. This decade also gave birth to numerous breeds of unprecedented radicalism, among which hedonism, militant feminism, multiculturalism, and moral relativism figure prominently. The effects of the sixties have now become the causes for still more radicalism. Over the past fifty years, and especially since the sixties, America has changed significantly in the degree to which it has lost its way. More than ever, the crowd apes the life-distorting images that abound on the ubiquitous television and upon the alluring cinema screen, images projected, in large part, by those who would exploit the gullibility of the common man and woman.

Were he alive in our time, how would Bell react, one might ask, to the sordid television talk show that celebrates abnormality or to the banal evening sitcom of our new millennium that panders to the basest sense of humor, or to the latest Hollywood productions that conjoin sex with sentimentality for the lachrymose? In all likelihood, he would respond as he did in his autobiographical book *Beyond Agnosticism:* "I find it hard, even yet, to embrace the way of the Virgin, but I was not very old before I knew that Astarte can be very stale." Today, the media continue to bombard us with salacious images—many of them violent—promoting the grand illusion that those who have amassed money and been graced with pretty faces are having sex practically all the time, in practically any place. What Bell said at the start of the last century is still true at the start of this one: "We are so naïvely delighted in having discovered that the Eternal made us men and women that we sometimes seem to be forgetting that He made us anything else."

Of course the media are not entirely to blame for the crowd's moral stupor. The crowd is finally responsible for itself, and ultimately accountable to God. Yet the signs of the time indicate that its appetite for the fleeting and momentary continues to grow ever more voracious as the new millennium dawns. What once seemed plenty, even to Bell's generation, now fails to satisfy. Today, for instance, the average family home contains more bedrooms and notably larger closets than the average home constructed fifty years ago, even though today's average family produces, by choice, fewer children than it did back then. While homes increase in size and boast more amenities, America itself grows seemingly smaller as communities further lose their autonomy, and as once diverse regions melt into a monotonous sameness.

This sameness organizes itself around an ideology that compels both husband and wife to work outside the home to amass products which Americans are convinced they must have to be happy and *au courant*. As a result, millions of children now spend their preschool years, if not their infancies, in institutional daycare centers, while their parents do exactly as they are disposed by the social engineers of modern liberalism. These engineers have been trying to reinvent society for the last century and a half. "Up until now philosophers have only interpreted the world," wrote their intellectual father, Karl Marx. "The point now is to change it."

A final few words ought to be devoted to changes in education. America's schools are not the same as they were when Bell denounced them, and the pedagogical facts and figures that were relevant at the time when Bell adduced them to bolster his claims about the demise of learning are, one must admit, dated and of little use to us today. Moreover, one has to admit that opportunities for learning are greater with the erection of more colleges and with the opening of their doors to those who might not have been admitted in times past. Furthermore, one would have to be obstinate not to acknowledge, with some obvious qualifications, the benefit of greater access to information via the Internet. Still, one might ask if education is any better now than in Bell's day. If one agrees with Bell that education must have a coherent framework and something timeless at its center, one is obliged to say no.

Here is not the place to rehearse all the problems that plague American education. But let us say just a word or two about the decay of reading. The educrat typically claims that more students are able to read today than in decades past, and he bases this claim on the fact that more high school students go on to college now than ever before. This claim has some validity—but very little. More students may be reading, but, owing to a lack of classroom rigor and proper instruction, they are not reading well. Evidence shows, and any reasonable teacher knows, that for high school and college students the level of reading comprehension is, on the average, lower now than when Bell taught school. Nor are students reading the right things. Rarely are they encouraged to engage the great books of the Western world. Instead, they are presented with demotic novels and plays that validate lifestyle choices.

What is more, students are also presented with the idea that one kind of experience is as valuable as another when it comes to reading. The experiential theorists who cultivate this idea insist that a student better "relates" to a poem or piece of fiction when he brings to it his own personal experience (no matter how provincial). They may be right, but they fail to see that there is more to reading books than relating to them on a personal level. One must wonder how the theorist could continue to promote this superficial kind of reading in the face of rampant cultural ignorance, when students grow ever less conversant with the seminal works that shaped the minds of those who founded their country. Are the theorists trying to occlude these works? What students ought to be bringing to literature are experiences of a literary kind. Students cannot fully appreciate a classic like *Heart of Darkness*, for example, unless they have some prior experience with Dante, whom Conrad invokes. Students become experienced readers, and good citizens to boot, by continually expanding their context for reading through encounters with texts that are morally and culturally significant.

If in the past five decades America's cultural and educational picture has changed in many ways for the worse, so has its religious life. Although churches have not entirely suppressed the proclamation of God's wisdom, they have nevertheless exiled just about all their prophets, or sequestered them in remote monasteries, or insisted that they make their message more pleasingly palatable for the crowd. One can certainly see why. Prophets have always been a disturbing bunch. They are forever pointing out ecclesiastical inconsistency and condemning deference to the world. They exact something from the laity instead of validating its way of life. Pride, ambition, the love of money, the lust for power—these they renounce and denounce with a disconcerting vigor. This has been the case from the dawn of Christendom, when the Twelve Apostles, whom most thought to be raging lunatics, went about turning the world on its head and unsettling the morally indifferent and the spiritually complacent. Men like Loyola and Luther and Wesley, in later times, were no more conducive to the status quo. The price that churches are paying today for preferring popularity to prophecy is amounting, as Bell predicted it would, to their becoming laughable as well as powerless.

Many things have changed since Bell took his stand against the follies of the last century. Yet his voice, as expressed in the following pages, can still resonate within contemporary America. More than ever its culture, now a crowd culture worshipping cellular gadgets and floating adrift in one virtual reality after another, needs to be grounded in genuine reality; it needs to be reoriented and humanized, and its citizens need to be dignified. Its schools desperately need rescuing from the ideologues who continue to alienate students from their intellectual heritage. Now more than ever, its faithful need to hear substantive sermons on those changeless truths concerning the creaturehood of mankind.

Crowd Culture reminds us that all this can be achieved, but only when those who share a common metaphysical dream "raise up rebels willing to pay the price which rebels must expect to pay." Only with the guidance of such a democratic elite can America hope to regain its sanity. Only under the leadership of those who have drunk deeply from the springs of our classical and Christian heritage can citizens come to know the real meaning of life, liberty, and justice for all. Only from example can Americans learn that, to avoid moral torpor, they must "seek to participate in the richness of tradition newly grasped, tradition reinterpreted." If America persists in its aimless course, its democracy can *only* end in catastrophe. Against those who now lead the way, the rebel must stand resolute. This is his "reasonable service," writes Bell, his "religious duty."

CICERO BRUCE
Professor of English
McMurry University

To
The Common Man

It is not the life of knowledge, not even if it includes all the sciences, that creates happiness and well-being, but a single branch of knowledge—the science of the good life. If you exclude this from the other branches, medicine will remain equally able to give us health, and shoemaking shoes, and weaving clothes; seamanship will continue still to save life at sea, and strategy to win battles; but without the knowledge of good and evil the use and excellence of these sciences will be found to have failed us.

—PLATO

Foreword

THE FOLLOWING CHAPTERS WERE LECTURES delivered in April, 1952, at Ohio Wesleyan University, on the Frederick Merrick Foundation. Dr. Merrick, one of the founders and an early president of that institution, gave a sum of money in 1889, the interest on which has since that date been used for a series of four lectures annually, on some subject having to do with "experimental and practical religion." This has been interpreted to include the relationship of religion and culture.

I am grateful to the president of Ohio Wesleyan University, Dr. Arthur S. Flemming, and to the Merrick Lecture Committee of the Faculty, for having extended to me the privilege of speaking to the ladies and gentlemen of the University. I only wish the lectures were more adequate, more worthy of the roster of fifty distinguished scholars who preceded me as Merrick Lecturers. All I could do was my labored best to deal with certain problems which I think need to be faced by those who love this country of ours and are more than a little alarmed about its present cultural complexion. Writing them has at least helped me to try to clarify my own thinking on this subject. I hope that they were of some small assistance to those who listened to them with such apparent interest, and to those who may do me the courtesy to read them.

God save our fatherland from its enemies, and chiefly from ourselves!

BERNARD IDDINGS BELL

I

The Cultural Picture

The spread of democracy will not necessarily help us, indeed it makes our task more difficult. To call the masses into power is to dilute existing culture. They must be humored and satisfied; attention must be paid to their interests and tastes and if these are trifling, ignoble and base, the level of civilization will fall. There is good democracy; there is also the democracy which is a social order in which a degenerate mass has no other care than to enjoy the ignoble pleasures of vulgar men.

—SIR RICHARD LIVINGSTONE

THE CHIEF THREAT TO AMERICA COMES FROM within America.

It comes from our prevailing self-admiration, from indisposition to listen to adverse criticism of our way of life, disinclination to see ourselves as we are, an unwill-ingness to confess our sins which has come dangerously near to being an inability to see that there are serious faults to admit and remedy. Most Americans regard an insis-tence on national self-criticism as traitorous or near it. In consequence, our people as a whole have acquired and re-tain a false optimism about the ability of our way of life to survive and flower. Most of us have a juvenile trust in the permanence of an America whose people forget the transitoriness of the immediate and the superficiality of the obvious, pay scarcely more than a polite lip service to what the race has discovered to be changeless and humanly necessary.

By no means all of us are complacent in this fashion. There is a growing number of critics, though still only a minority of Americans belong to it, which sees not only that all is far from well in these United States but that what is wrong is more than incidental or accidental. This minority is as well aware as anyone can be of American virtues and abilities. It knows that we are competent to make, cheaply and for the most part well, almost any-thing we wish to make; and that we are as a nation incred-ibly, though not inexhaustibly, wealthy. It knows, too, that Americans are hospitable, kindly, generous, though they are usually unwilling to involve themselves, in order to assist others, in sacrifice which means pain. The mi-nority is sure that our way of life is better than that which prevails in totalitarian countries, if for no other reason than that criticism of that which is is tolerated in our land if anyone cares to go in for it, reluctantly tolerated but still tolerated.

But somehow or other more than a few of us begin to see that while wealth accumulates in these United States, man seems to decay. Corruption corrodes our political and industrial doings. In our private lives a pervading relativ-ism, an absence of conviction about what is the good life, a willingness to seek the easy way rather than the way of integrity, blunts the proddings of conscience, takes the zest out of living, creates a general boredom. We are not a happy people; our alleged gaiety is not spontaneous. Our boredom results not only in a reluctant morality but in shockingly bad manners, which most of us do not even know are bad manners. We become increasingly trucu-lent. Our way of life, while opulent and brash and super-ficially friendly, is less and less conducive to peace of mind and security of soul.

The minority which feels this way grows in numbers, in clarity of perception, in willingness to speak up even when to do so brings down on its head a clamorous scorn from those who flatter and exploit an ailing democracy and, not too rarely, mete out persecution in its name.

The critical group of patriotic malcontents is sure that what the United States must produce, if it is to manage our magnificent material achievement, is Americans who are more sane, more spiritually adequate, than the present crop. We need such Americans not only to prevent us becoming and remaining slaves here at home to an industrial and political machinery manipulated by the unscrupulous, nor merely to keep us from greedily snarling over the fruits of technology until we find ourselves at one another's throats. The critical minority knows that we must produce and educate more understanding and more spiritually adequate Americans if we are to insure even our survival as a people and protect from external attack those opportunities for freedom in an ordered society which our Founding Fathers envisioned and for which they made great sacrifices.

The minority recognizes that in the One World which is coming into being our nation cannot long secure itself from alien enemies if all it has to depend on is a continued threat to use armed force or an attempt to purchase global good will toward us. It knows, for instance, that

Charles Malik, the Lebanese Minister to Washington, told the unvarnished truth in an address which he made not long ago in New York City. "In world affairs," he said, "there are two serious handicaps which it is difficult for the United States to live down. In massiveness, the old world has a decided advantage over the new, both as to population and to sheer quantity in matter. In time, therefore, the old world will certainly overtake you on the material plane. The second disadvantage is that whereas there are cultural and racial continuities between the Soviet Union and the whole of Asia, there are no such continuities between the United States and Asia. This is one of the most destiny-bearing facts of the world situation today. The only way for America to overcome these two disadvantages is by concentration on quality." "Can the United States develop," Dr. Malik asked, "a type of man who sums up in his character such a quality of understanding, of humility, of truth, of humor, of moral stature, of strength and resourcefulness of mind, of pregnant ideas, of universal sympathy and friendship and love, as to enable him, by the sheer weight of his being, to overcome the disadvantages of mass and discontinuity? It has not yet dawned upon America how much is required of her to develop this kind of humanity."

It is, of course, impossible to indict a whole nation; but by and large Americans are not today the sort of people whom Dr. Malik rightly says we need to be. Our dangerous inadequacy is due not so much to deliberate iniquity on the part of individuals as to the compulsions of a culture which shoots wide of the mark in its estimate of human values.

A culture is that complex of attitudes and resultant actions in which are embodied and revealed the prevailing aspirations and desires of that congeries of human beings in the midst of which one lives. It is exceedingly difficult for anyone to escape the pressure of public opinion. It is hard to free oneself from it even in matters of minor and incidental importance. In a democracy like ours it is, indeed, commonly considered unforgivable to wish so to escape. But there must be those who know freedom from the clamorous crowd if there is to be any considerable improvement in the complexion of the common life. To better American character there must be those who understand the prevailing American culture; those who have discovered what ends our citizens chiefly pursue and train their children to pursue, and what means of pursuing these ends are deemed respectable. If the ends seem inadequate or the means reprehensible when viewed and evaluated in the light of the agelong history of human behavior, the patriot must reject and attack them, no matter at what risk to himself. He must refuse to swim with the current for the sake of popularity or ease.

The shrewd examination and stout resistance required make demands which are almost invariably too great for the intelligence and fortitude of the Common Man. He needs to be led by those who are more than usually percipient and courageous. Social reformation never originates with majorities. Always there must be those who have the wit and the temerity to oppose the majorities—a difficult and dangerous procedure. The least useful of would-be patriots is he who, when he knows better, uncritically conforms to the mores and condones such conformity on the ground that it is "democratic" to run with the pack whithersoever the pack desires to run. There must be those who resist our culture, the present culture of the Common Man.

One hears a great deal about "the American way of life"; but what does the phrase mean? Ask this question of the next twenty-five people you talk with and you will get almost as many variant answers. Probably most of those you ask will never have taken the trouble to define it. Some of them will be sure to regard you with suspicion. Because you insist on knowing what the American way of life is, you are supposed to be against it, whatever it is; you are probably a Fascist or a Communist or some such reprobate. One or two may tell you to go read the Declaration of Independence and the Constitution, forgetting that these deal with a way of government rather than a way of life. The suggested inquiry may be full of surprises for you, may amuse you, possibly may shock you into realization of the moral confusion of the American mind.

The culture that determines our way of life is a generalization of the definitions of proper and fruitful objectives that are held by the usual American and of his actions resultant therefrom. This generalization reflects us. It reveals what notions prevail in the United States about the nature of the good life and how to come at it.

But are there not, perhaps, many cultures existing side by side in America? One hears it said occasionally that the chief problem in this country is one of cultural multiplicity. Is it not a melting pot for those who hold dear many ways of life which originated in other lands: the culture of Great Britain, that of Ireland, that of Northern Europe, that of the Mediterranean countries, that of the Near East, that of the Far East, the many cultures of Africa? This notion of various ways of life as yet not fused, or slowly fusing, once did have some foundation in fact; but this is not so any more, at least not to a significant degree. We have grown beyond the end-of-the-century comparison of many cultures being boiled up in a caldron of Anglo-Saxon origin. The contents of the pot have been so well melted by now that points of difference have become incidental. Nor has the residuum taken on the complexion of the pot, as many thought it would. The pot itself has been melted up, largely, lost in the amalgam. Our way of life is not predominantly Anglo-Saxon, not any more; neither is it the confused and confusing sort of jumble which a half century ago many feared it would become.

Nor do we have much left of geographical diversities of culture in these United States. There was a time when it meant something to speak of the culture of New England or the culture of New York or Virginian culture or that of the Middle West or that of Texas or that of California. A few faint and accidental differences linger on here and there; but the formerly substantial variations are mostly outgrown. Life is essentially evaluated nowadays much the same way in Atlanta and Spokane; in Richmond, Virginia, and Richmond, Indiana; in Portland, Oregon, and Portland, Maine; in Chicago and Philadelphia and New Orleans; in Milwaukee and Manhattan and Miami. The country is all of a piece. This is why to many foreign visitors the United States seems to be, as one of them once put it, "a homogeneity, so united as to be monotonous."

Nor do cultures vary greatly in the United States according to occupational or class backgrounds: rural and urban and suburban, agricultural or technological. There is among us no peculiarly bourgeois culture; everyone is bourgeois. There is no proletarian culture as distinct from middle-class culture; the two have become indistinguishable. And there are only faint traces left of that culture which once characterized the older elite. Those who have a hankering for old-fashioned patrician pleasures find it easier to go in for them mostly alone, secret drinkers of that which flows from classic springs, with just enough of the real thing in the potation to make it smell and taste a little as of yore, but adulterated with crude spirits for the sake of a popular kick. This is not the place to deplore these changes or to praise them; our present business is to understand and describe.

The children in American schools stand every day with one hand on the heart and the other stretched out toward the flag and say that they are pledged to serve an America which is "one and indivisible." This is not an aspiration any more; the oath involves only a statement of simple fact. We have moralized, unified, equalized, standardized our country from the Atlantic to the Pacific, from Canada to Mexico. This may turn out to be a blessing or it may turn out to be a curse; but at any rate it makes American life much easier for the thoughtful to examine and evaluate than was the case at the turn of the century, easier too for the unthinking to accept that which is with an unchallenging complacency. America is a very large country but its cultural pattern is single, becomes more so every day.

The way of life in any culture is revealed not by what is emotionally said or written about it by the boastful or by the scolding, but through examination of certain indexes. Among the ones usually relied on by social scientists as most revealing are the press (with its modern variants, radio and television); books and magazines commonly read; advertising; sports and recreation; music; the pictorial arts; the theater, including again the movies, radio and television; divorce and the permanency of the home; good or bad manners, including general attitudes toward disorder and noise; education and its objectives; religion and the concern or lack of esteem in which it is held. If anyone examines such indexes dispassionately, objectively, he will speedily discover what is the American way of life in these mid-century years. He will come to understand what the pressures are which have most to do with making him and you and me and the neighbors and the children what we all are, the pressures from which there is no chance of easy escape for anyone who believes in the sovereign rightness of the multitude. To understand our culture no special shrewdness is required—only honest observations of the indexes.

Read the newspapers, for instance. There are not more than a dozen of them among the thousands of local journals which show independent character or integrity, or which indicate a reading public that it would pay one to trust with his wallet, his wife, or his good name. Observe what they regard as the news that is important, the news that deserves to be featured; how gossip and scandal and crime and sensation are played up. See, also, how like as buttons they are in the way they tell what is happening nationally or internationally, and why it is happening. Most of the extra-local news is collected and distributed by syndicated agencies, agencies which can color the material just about as their governors may desire, by virtue of which fact American opinion and action are manageable as truly as in any censor-controlled totalitarian state, perhaps more effectively than in such a state because the reader in this country thinks he is perusing independent journals while, with rare exceptions, he is not. His suspicion of being manipulated is thereby lulled.

One interesting and typical example may be worth recalling. When Russia was Hitler's ally in World War II, the American people were told by the papers, and believed, that the Russians were little short of fiends. Suddenly Russia changed sides. For reasons not too credible either to her or to us, she became our ally. At a dinner in New York at that time, I sat next to a high-up officer of one of the great news-collecting agencies. "I suppose," I ventured, "now that the Muscovites are on our side, the American people will have to be indoctrinated so as to stop thinking of them as devils and begin to regard them as noble fellows." "Of course," he replied. "We know what our job is in respect to that. We of the press will bring about a complete and almost unanimous *volte face* in the belief of the Common Man about the Russians. We shall do it within three weeks." He was right about it. The papers, fed by the news agencies, did just that; and in less time than he said it would take we were cheering for Papa Stalin and the Politburo who were, we now felt sure, liberty-loving democrats and entirely trustworthy. What extraordinary power! As Lord Acton said, "Power corrupts and absolute power absolutely corrupts." The point here is merely to note that we are led about by the press, and with what ease.

Notice, too, how brazenly the press violates proper rights to privacy, even in cases of deep sorrow or pitiable weakness; how it encourages its readers to be Peter Prys and Peeping Toms. See especially how it vulgarizes the nobilities inherent in marriage, in birth, in death. Consider, too, how the news columns plainly imply that next to nobody makes or sells or plans or says or does things, except for money or applause. And do not forget the page or two or three or four of what are fondly called "comic strips," the fiction of the Common Man, whereby he and his wife and his children revel sometimes in vulgarity, more often in sentimentality, more often still in sheer inanity,

endlessly drawn out. None of these degradations of jour-
nalism would be indulged in for a moment if it were not
that most of our people are delighted with such stuff.

As for weekly and monthly publications, there are
very few of them which a maturely self-respecting citizen, if he thought about it, would let into his house through
the front door, or even the back door. Most of the few of
them that are reasonably decent, including a few with
honorable pasts, keep trembling on the verge of bank-
ruptcy. The ones of these which manage to hold their
own or better, have to attract circulation by mixing with
material of worth and wit and wisdom a great deal of other
material that is shoddy rubbish if not worse, adding sen-
sationalism and scandal for the many to an ever-lessening
provision of sanity for the few. Of one of the best of the
lot—it has a prodigious circulation—it has been truly said,
"In every issue there is learning and lubricity, piety and
pornography, and all of it decorated with astoundingly
good photographs."

No one should make the mistake of supposing that
our periodicals and their visual extensions, the radio and
television, are what they are because devil-inspired publishers and broadcasters set out to degrade us. The producers and circulators, as a matter of fact, are frequently
ashamed of their product but excuse themselves by saying
that publishing and broadcasting are not longer to be re-

garded as honorable professions. Each is to be looked at as a business. The things they put out are what they are because we, the customers, are the kind of people we are and will buy nothing more reputable, at least in large enough quantity to bring in to the owners a sure and considerable profit. They print and broadcast what will build up mass circulation and so secure advertising, from which alone comes any large return on their investments. Surely, they insist, no reasonable American can fault them for being so typically American. Is not selection and presentation of news and entertainment entitled to the benefit of such free enterprise as theirs? Would it not be foolish to disregard the public, which is made up, as Mr. Barnum once said, of "one born every minute"?

Read the papers, then, daily and weekly and monthly, and get a notion of the folks who buy them. It is these purchasers who in the aggregate are our country, our state, our city, our neighborhood. You may also get new light on what you yourself have become or are becoming.

When one looks at books, another cultural index, one may again find oneself upset in one's notion of the culture which molds us and our children, especially if one has been accustomed to believe this culture essentially healthy and only incidentally ill.

It would be foolish to aver that there are not a good many worthwhile books being written, published, read, perhaps as many as at any time in our history; but the point is that the Common Man does not read them. He reads something quite different. In former days a liberally educated minority bought books and read them; the rest, if not enlightened by letters, were not corrupt in respect to them. They did not extol trash, and worse than trash, as reputable literature. Nowadays Demos, having learned to read, reveals an infantile taste by what he reads, the greater part of it rubbish and not a little of it garbage.

Poetry, criticism, the essay, are not to Demos' taste. Fiction is what he goes in for, and such fiction! The publishers know what Demos will buy in quantity. He and his wife seek distraction from the dullness of a daily, weekly, monthly, yearly routine that has largely depersonalized them, a diet from which the vitamins have been eliminated. What Demos and his Lady desire is escape from monotony. They are looking for stories that are essentially romantic, stories that will help them forget a probably comfortable but somehow stuffy round. They welcome almost any kind of romance.

It is not merely the sword-and-dagger variety that attracts them, or the boy-meets-girl type. Realism of the most violent and sordid kind is even more satisfyingly romantic to readers whose days are too devitalized for normal enjoyments! Even the blood-and-guts of battle is romantic to read about for those who have never had to endure it. War novels are not much read by veterans. If violence is one of the chief characteristics of a potential best-seller, another is such eroticism as will enable Demos and his Lady to get away from conventionally domestic sex and go in vicariously for a lewdness which they are ashamed, or afraid, or too emotionally tired to indulge in firsthand. They dearly love to read about sex in the raw. And if a manuscript comes along which is both brutal and lustful, it is doubly certain of a large sale.

The most popular novelist in America today, if one may judge by the number of copies sold, is a meretricious brute of a fellow, almost ludicrously savage in his substance and his style. He writes tales of a violence that is near to madness plus a degenerate sexuality. His best-selling production reaches its climax when a woman, physically beautiful and fascinatingly wicked, undresses herself, with an almost incredible particularity of lascivious description, in the presence of a libidinous and savage hero. When she is quite bare, the hero shoots her twice in the belly. As she dies, she cries, "How could you?" He replies, "It was easy." End of the book. Over 1,200,000 copies of this masterpiece have been purchased. The sale of all his books, essentially the same in plot with minor differences of decoration, has passed the 10,000,000 mark in four years. This pander is indeed an exceptionally low creature, but he is at the moment the Common Man's delight. He has lots of imitators. Many of the more suave novels of the book clubs are not much better than his. And it has some significance that with rare exception the cheap paper-bound novels which clutter up every drug-store and railway bookstall carry lurid and pornographic cover pictures, even when the books themselves are not as wholly disreputable as many of them are. Violence plus sexosity equals sales.

Our popular literature reveals that our fellow citizens desire to escape from life as it is lived among us into a dream world of brutality and carnality, desire it with a passionate intensity which makes them buy in large quantity fiction much of which is worse than disreputable. A few books even yet, few among the many that are printed, are designed to be read by literate and decent people; most of the product of press and bindery is escapist trash. This fact certainly has cultural significance, especially in a society where the Common Man determines life patterns to the extent that he does in America.

Look at another index. Americans are immensely concerned with amusement; but their desire is not so much to amuse themselves as to be amused by someone else. Take music, for instance. Despite a growth in musical appreciation in this century which has been more than considerable, though perhaps it has not been so great as is sometimes supposed, we do not make nearly as much music today as our grandparents did. Instead, we are content to sit back and listen to someone else make music for us. Perhaps we are too lazy to sing and play instruments. Perhaps we are unwilling to go through the discipline necessary to acquire musical facility. Perhaps we are overawed by professional expertness, unaware that much more enjoyment is gained by singing or playing oneself, even though one does it badly, than from hearing it done, however perfectly. Our musical experience is largely receptive, not creative.

The same is true of other arts. We do not, for example, make or decorate our homes or the objects of common use within them, not to the extent that our grandparents did, and got great joy from it. We buy what mass producers tell us is in the best taste. It may or may not be good; but it is not ours, no matter how much we pay for it. Neither in creating nor arranging things domestic do we find much self-expression. The drama, too, we relegate to professionals whose performances we pay to look at, not often in a theater (for we have killed the theater by extravagance and exploitation) but at the motion pictures or over the radio and television. We write or produce or act next to no plays ourselves; and most of us, and our children, would rather be caught dead than observed playing charades or reciting monologues. Even general conversation, which to be amusing always involves dramatic give and take, has become nearly a lost art.

This same misfortune has overtaken what used to be the greatest American amusement of them all, the art called athletics. We are not really a sporting people, not any more. We do not, most of us, play games; we watch them. Our idea of sport is to buy seats in a stadium and look at paid gladiators do combat while we applaud them or abuse them or wager on them. The scandals of late in what used to be, and still purports to be, amateur sport, have not been caused by wicked betting rings. There would be no betting rings, no bribery by them, if it were not for the fact that we have sunk from a sporting activity into a sporting passivity. We would rather bet on a winner than contend. As long as this remains true of us, as it was not of our fathers, athletes will be subsidized and games fixed.

Another index of culture is the degree to which profession of political principles is or is not matched by responsible action. In respect to this, the situation in America reveals a good deal. We say that we believe in the rightness of majority rule, with due protection of the rights of minorities, all this made effective by law duly enacted and enforced by elected representatives. As a matter of fact, however, a large part of our people is unwilling to participate in such government, even to the extent of casting ballots at election time. In the Presidential contest in 1948, for example, 48,836,579 voted; but that year there was a minimum of 94,704,000 eligible to vote. Half the electorate stayed away from the polls. Similar proportion prevails when lesser or more local officers than President are being chosen. In elections for membership in Congress, the percentage of nonparticipation sometimes runs to as high as 70 per cent.[1]

Our people apparently do not care to take the trouble to help govern themselves or to choose their governors. Or else, it may be, they feel incompetent to judge the issues at stake, never having learned at home or in school how to judge anything. Or else they are of the opinion that no party or politician is better or worse than his or its rivals, that all politicians are rascals and all party platforms dishonest. These impressions may or may not be justified. This is not the place to argue that out. The significant thing to note here is the evident popular opinion that "politics and politicians are rotten" and that the citizens generally can do nothing about it. Or else they may suppose that it does not much matter who holds office since the real governors, they feel sure, are the lobbies of pressure groups which tell the officeholders, from the President and Congress down to the most humble bailiff, what is to be done, and when, to whom and not to whom.

The evident discrepancy between political theory and political action must alarm those who believe in our kind of democracy. The cultural indication is twofold. First, it would seem that most of us have such small respect for the body politic that we do not feel it worth while to bother about who are entrusted with the making or enforcement of the laws. Secondly, it reveals that a majority of us, a constantly growing majority, is willing to talk one way and act another, in respect to a basic human activity like government, with a nonchalance that is not even cynical.

Another index not to be ignored is the degree to which residence is stable or otherwise. If families frequently move about, there are soon too little of those mutual connections which come from neighborly interrelationships.

What is a civilized man? By derivation of the word, he is one who lives and thinks in a city. The Greek city, the medieval city, the American city as it was before industrialization brought about huge agglomerations of urban population, was a community, a constant group of families each of which, and each of whose members, had a stake in the common welfare and was not permitted to forget it. Such a city was large enough for reasonable self-expression but small enough for public influence on behavior. One had not merely to obey the statute law or go to jail, but also the customs, the unwritten law, or be sent to Coventry. For a city to function, its population has to be not too great, and stable from year to year, if possible from generation to generation.

The late W. N. Guthrie used to say there was no civilized man or woman in New York City who had not been civilized somewhere else, in a small town on the plains, in the ghetto in Warsaw, on a southern plantation, somewhere like that. New York, he maintained, could civilize nobody for, while in that megalopolis there is opportunity to express oneself all over the map, there is next to no neighborhood opinion to exercise correction. There are, in fact, no neighborhoods, only frequently migrating human units, anarchs, so lonely that they will gladly follow any demagogic quack who pretends to be friendly. This was exaggeration, but not greatly so. With us the *mores* are no longer determined by mutual consent among friends. They are built up mechanically and anonymously; and because they are what they are, they no longer help as of yore. We still more or less obey statute law; we pay little heed to unwritten customs of mutual dignity, or even of decency. This is now true not only in such monstrosities as New York or Chicago or Detroit or Los Angeles or Houston but in much smaller places. Thanks to the frequent migration of vast segments of our people, all our cities have ceased to civilize, have ceased to be communities.

In such a situation it is not unnatural that individuals should live more and more each for self, with less and less consideration for the comfort, even for the safety, of the people next door or the family over the way. One does not know their names. Why bother to learn? They will soon be moving, or one will move oneself. After years of this there remains in America little regard for the rights of others to privacy or peace. Let the radio blast. Let the children yell. Throw the rubbish where you will. The sanctity of property, either communal or personal, becomes nobody's proper concern. In New York City, for example, children in 1951 caused wanton damage to school property—windows, fences, tile, furniture, equipment, works of art—which it cost the taxpayers over $500,000 to replace.[2] Such vandalism is matched, in proportion to population, in hundreds of other municipalities. As for private property other than one's own, litter it, maul and deface it, walk off with it, make it necessary for the owners to keep it under lock and key; while open lawns and flower beds have become a nostalgic memory for many who once lived in a civilized fashion.

No such degeneration could happen if we were not a restlessly migratory folk. This index reveals a fundamental weakness in our way of life, one which cannot be ignored.

It does not seem too necessary further to conduct a guided tour into American culture. The indexes are at hand for anyone to use. It is only necessary to insist that they must not be disregarded by him who would see what our way of life is actually like. Let us not make the mistake of supposing that American culture of today is the culture of America a hundred years ago or fifty or twenty or ten. Nor is it the culture of the few which matters. It is the culture of the many that is American culture. This is the age of the Common Man. We may admire him as the only true gentleman or reject him as a stupid bounder or, with greater justice, look on him as one whose economic emancipation has gone on faster than he has been able constructively to assimilate it. However we regard him, we must know him for what he is. This is where the indexes help. What the Common Man's culture is worth, is another question.

What opinion of all this is held today by the small but growing critical minority of whom we were speaking at the beginning of this chapter? That minority is fairly well persuaded that no culture such as the indexes reveal will produce the kind of men and women who can long keep our people happy or our country competent to survive in the world as it is coming to be.

The first thing that strikes this critical minority, as it looks at the whole cultural picture, is that ours is a nation of new-rich people, well washed, all dressed up, rather pathetically unsure just what it is washed and dressed up for; a nation convinced that a multitude of material goods, standardized, furiously and expensively advertised by appeals to greed and vanity, will in themselves make life worth the living. Because we are new-rich, we overvalue possessions. Almost any individual who makes a great deal of money very rapidly supposes that mere possession of wealth is evidence of worth. He also is apt to imagine that with his means he can buy happiness. These mistakes usually seem folly to the old-rich, to one who was born to property, whose father and mother were bred with it. Such a one knows that merely because he or his friends have it, is no sign that they are worth it, but quite commonly the contrary. He has learned through experience that money is not in itself very valuable stuff. Happiness, which is what all men desire, cannot be purchased; it is an illusive something not for sale. The old-rich know these things well enough, but the new-rich rarely discover them until they too have grown accustomed to possessions. So it seems to be with our society. We go in, almost without question and in all classes, for the sordid nonsense of supposing that externalities possessed ennoble the owners, that a full fist invariably indicates a fine spirit.

The second conviction on which our culture is based seems to be this, that animal appetites are mighty and to be sacrificed unto if we would enjoy a satisfactory existence; and the chief of all the appetites is sex. Our stage, our music, our dancing, our books and magazines, our advertising, our dress, strike strenuously an exaggerated note of sex appeal. We have even devised a popular moral philosophy based upon the supposition that, if one refuses to indulge sexual appetites, he or she is in danger of the madhouse. No reputable psychiatrist gives such advice to his clients; but we go for our psychology not to him but to the editor of the tabloid newspaper. No one will deny that sex is important; but it is not so centrally important as most of us seem to suppose. Man is a sexual animal; but he is a great deal more than that.

Our culture, in the third place, seems based upon a conviction that to be comfortable is utterly indispensable if man is to fulfill his destiny. It occurs only to exceptional people that the whole cult of comfort is petty, ignoble, unworthy of human nature, absurd. All too few ask whether it can possibly be that, since our primeval ancestors crawled from the slime of the sea, first the animal world and then the human race have struggled on, at cost of travail and pain and tears and death, merely that modern man may sit down and be comfortable.

The fourth impulse back of our cultural endeavors and achievements seems to be a ridiculous notion that whether a man be good or bad, wise or foolish, matters less than that he should conform to pattern. The pattern to which we are expected to conform is that set by the overgrown and depersonalized megalopolis. We shall say more later on about the growth of this conformity.

And fifth, our crowd-mindedness renders us suggestible, manipulatable, easy meat for almost any propagandist who is willing to flatter, to encourage animality, to promise ease and opulence with a minimum of labor expended to get them, and freedom from responsibility.

"Well, what of it?" someone asks. "If the culture we have is the culture we like, then it is what we like. Where is the harm as long as we approve of ourselves, which we most certainly do? And are not the other nations envious of us for the very things your critical minority calls our defects?" A word or two about each of these questions may be in order.

Do other peoples envy us? The answer, as may be discovered by any open-minded traveler, is that they have little or no desire to become like us in anything except technological know-how. They usually regard us otherwise with condescension mixed with dread that somehow or other we may overthrow what they regard as a better way of life and degrade them to our cultural level. This is no exaggeration. Not only is it so in Western Europe; it is the mood in Russia, in most of Asia and the Near East, in Latin America from the Rio Grande to Cape Horn. They look on our concern for size, speed, new models every year, as more than a little childish. They consider our effulgent and stentorian advertising both wasteful and ridiculous. They know too much about our restlessness. They see how our very mass production is preventing the joys of craftsmanship. They laugh at our hysterical enthusiasm for sports in which we take no part. They deplore our indifference to ideas and our disrespect for continuity and tradition. They sense in us tremendous power without our having any clear notion of what we desire to do with that power. They are afraid of us more than they admire us. They love us not. Is it conducive to a proper happiness or to our safety, that we should be held in such general disesteem?

"Where is the harm," the other question puts it, "if what we are suits us?" The harm lies in this, that down the ages no people whose compelling culture has been based on greed for goods, on avidity for sensation, on search for enervating comforts, on conformity to a type set by subhuman urbanization, on a divorcement of the people from the soil, on eager response to the flatteries of propagandists, ever has managed to exist very long. Our wrong emphases are acids which dissolve the social cements. Unsureness about what life is for eventually brings about ineffectiveness in all departments of living, after a while even in technological proficiency. Then, to cure an alarming disorder, in rides the Man on Horseback with plausible oversimplifications.

If we are to rescue America from Americans, we shall have to raise up a new generation which will live less immaturely. This can happen only if Demos recovers from his present self-applauding jamboree, only if once more he comes to know the comparative values of human living as the race has learned them down the millennia. As we stand revealed by candid examination of the indexes, our culture is childish. If we go on as we are, we shall not produce the kind of citizens necessary for America's continued happiness or safety. We shall not bring forth "a type of man who sums up in his character a quality of understanding, of humility, of truth, of humor, or moral stature, of strength and resourcefulness of mind, of pregnant ideas, of universal sympathy and friendship and love." If we and our children must live out our days in the sort of culture that the indexes indicate, can anything be done by us and for us in the circumstances? If nothing can be done to arrest disintegration, then how can those of us live happily who know what it means to be effectively human?

II

The School

I know no safe depository of the ultimate powers of society but the people themselves; and if we think them not enlightened enough to exercise their control with a wholesome discretion, the remedy is not to take it from them but to inform their discretion by education.

—Thomas Jefferson

How can we develop americans of the kind needed for our survival, Americans who can rescue us from a present inadequacy not in technology, where we are beyond praise, but in our inner selves? There are two social institutions to which it is common to turn with trust that they will surely produce the necessary sort of citizens, namely, the School and the Church; but quite a few of us are not too certain that either of these, as we now have it, is sufficient to provide the sort of manhood and womanhood we lack and are in danger because we lack. Is it just possible, some of us ask, that both the School and the Church have been themselves too corrupted by American culture to train those who will resist and reform the temper of the times? In this chapter let us look at the School, try to see why it is not doing a better job, consider what might be done to make it effective in producing more sane, more adequate Americans. In the next chapter, we can similarly consider the Church.

There is justification for American pride in its system of public education. Our fathers wisely concluded that a democracy can properly function only if its citizens are enough educated for them to handle an industrial, governmental, cultural machinery; and we continue to set ourselves to the tasks involved. The job has become gigantic. There are over 29,000,000 children between six and sixteen years of age who are under instruction in elementary schools and high schools, and over 1,000,000 teachers who look after them. Nearly 1,250,000 more are teaching or studying in institutions of higher learning. These persons constitute almost one-fifth the total population of the United States. No nation else, now or in the past, has kept such a proportion of its people under instruction for so long or spent such tremendous sums trying to fit them for mature and fruitful living.

We are told by most of those who administer this vast education system that the effort has succeeded, is succeeding, will continue more and more to succeed, in turning out a competent citizenry; that the quality of the schools has kept pace with their growth in numbers. Those who do the actual teaching are by no means sure about this, and those who must deal with the product are not wholly persuaded either.

There are a good many honest doubters who simply cannot say "How true" to such a confident dictum, for instance, as that of Columbia Professor Henry Steele Commager, writing in *Life* October 16, 1950. He says, "For a century and a half American schools served and strengthened the commonwealth. They provided a citizenry as enlightened as any on earth. They justified and vindicated democracy's promise.... They will justify that faith in the future as they have in the past." Possibly so, but again possibly not. Even Mr. Commager has doubts about it, a few of which he more than hints at toward the end of that generally eulogistic article of his. And although he does not mention it, he knows, for he is one of our leading scholars in American history, that in many respects the schools which we have now are quite a different kettle of fish from those which helped develop the men and women who settled, defined and developed this country.

The older schools were community controlled, quickly responsive to parental desires, not anonymous. They were in constant and healthy local competition with one another in ideas, disciplines, methods. The schools of today are standardized, conventionalized, more alike every year, and this because American education has become to an unhealthy extent a large-scale government monopoly.

There is more than a suspicion in the minds of many competent observers that, because of increased standardization and more predominating state supervision, our schools are in danger of being directed by bureaucratic theorists who are distant from the realities involved in local and particular situations. Because schools are tied up with political appointment and tenure, this has dubious possibilities. The surest way to corrupt a genuine democracy is to place its educational facilities under a bureaucracy of experts who are apt to think entirely too well of those who, having gained control of political machinery, pay the pedagogues their salaries out of tax funds. The alleged educational experts are often flattered by the government. They frequently do not know to what sinister ends their well-meant theoretical policies can be put. Local criticism has been silenced and the teachers have little or no protection for their freedom. When at last they find this out, it is too late to revolt. Let an educator advocate something which does not follow the current party line, and see his sorry fate. Once government controls the schools, it becomes ever easier through education to fool all the people all of the time, easier than it once was to fool part of the people part of the time. In the larger and larger scale of organization of our schools there is a danger that the schools will become little more than propaganda agencies, used to sell the people a nasty piece of goods.

Encroachments are already more than apparent on such a degree of local self-determination of the schools as is necessary to develop and continue a healthy popular criticism of elected rulers and of those classes and pressure groups which manipulate the selection and retention of our rulers. Such coercions are hard to resist, especially when we have undertaken an educational program so expensive that soon only tax-levying Washington will be able to assume financial responsibility for it. Nine-tenths of all the teachers in elementary schools and high schools are today paid out of tax funds so insufficient as to cry aloud for federal assistance; nor can adequate buildings and equipment be procured without heavy subsidy by the national government.

Financing is done and control exerted, be it repeated, less and less by local communities. They have not the money. They have little to tax for school purposes except real and personal property. Such taxes are not sufficient. The larger part of modern taxable wealth does not consist in real property. Much of our possessions, too, is corporately held, and the greater part of industry and business is anything but local. More and more the schools cry out for money from the Federal Treasury, for Washington alone has opportunity to raise the necessary money by levies on aggregations of capital, on enterprises widely owned and widely operating. Whether we like the idea or not, in the future more and more of the bill for education is going to have to be paid by Washington.

This is dangerous, for the simple reason that he who pays the piper calls the tune. When a government gives money to schools it more and more insists, regardless of the rights of minorities or peculiarities of locality or variance in legitimate opinion, philosophic or political or economic or religious, on control of the programs and studies which are paid for with the funds which it bestows. Politicians do not refrain, because of the nature of politics they cannot refrain, from trying to dictate what is to be taught and what not, how it may be taught and how not, to whom it may be taught and to whom not. They maintain and frequently honestly believe that it is their bounden duty to do precisely this. "These professors and other teachers are dangerous if left free from governmental supervision." It soon comes to pass that able administrators, outstanding scholars, great instructors, are sure of holding their jobs only if their ideas, writings, speeches, procedures, conform to the prejudices of whatever happens to be the group that maintains in power a prevailing political faction. American teaching already begins to find itself more and more tied up in red-tape absentee imposed, and then dictated to.

In this respect at least, the schools of today are not much like those earlier schools which helped make the free and nonconformist men and women who founded America and developed it in the eighteenth and nineteenth centuries.

There are other significant differences. The aim of the older schools was primarily to turn out men and women who could think, confident that those who were trained to think could be trusted on their own to look after problems of adjustment, individual and social; but the more modern schools go on the theory that it is their business themselves to bring about such adjustments, only secondarily to concern themselves with developing pupils in the art of thinking. The older schools, again, founded and run by Christians, encouraged and imparted Christian spiritual entrustments and Christian morals. Today these cannot legally be taught, or recommended, by the public schools to which 88 per cent of American children go, go because there are no other schools for them to attend. Schools built on a Christian philosophy were one thing; schools built on John Dewey's philosophy or on any other relativistic philosophy are something else again, and are only too likely to produce alumni who have no definite standards of right and wrong, who judge words and deeds only by whether they seem expedient in a given, temporary, set of circumstances. In character education such schools do not much resemble their predecessors which helped make our democracy function in earlier decades.

For all these reasons it by no means follows that because the older schools made competent Americans, the present schools, which reject most of the foundations on which the older schools were built, will do an equally satisfactory job, a job conducive to the survival of that which the Fathers built and which their educational system deliberately fostered. The modern school is not, then, a natural development of the schools of a hundred years ago or even fifty years ago. The system as it is now is something new, largely a product of that twentieth century which has made so many blunders. To say that it is new is not necessarily to imply that it is better. It must in any event be judged not by its alleged ancestry but by the effectiveness of its contemporary product.

Is that product to be trusted morally and spiritually to regenerate a decadent America? A good many observers, believers in public education, think that it is not. These critics—their number increases with every year—are reluctantly of the opinion that the alumni now being turned out are incompetent for the most part to think and act intelligently or bravely in this difficult era, unable to understand themselves or their society, easily victimized by propaganda devices manipulated by the unscrupulous. These critics are not to be ignored. They are not disgruntled troublemakers. Most of them are adversely critical solely because they needs must deal with those who have been subjected to the schools. They find that to do this is neither pleasant nor reassuring. These many observers are sure that notwithstanding all the virtues of our educational development, and they are many, the public school at present may on the whole be harmful as well as helpful. This impression takes form in various charges, but most of the critics agree that the following are among the things that are most seriously wrong:

The first charge is that there is neglect of proper drill in the use of words—in reading and writing and speaking and listening; in the use of number not only as a tool for making things, doing things, but as an instrument to develop powers of abstracting and generalizing; in perception of form, in such observation of the size, shape, texture of physical objects as enables one to distinguish between facts and inaccurate guesses. Without a developed facility in these disciplines thought remains sloppy, intercommunication defective, action largely emotional. It does not matter what various information a child, or a grown person for that matter, may accumulate, so these critics insist, unless that child or that grown person has mastered these intellectual disciplines as well as his native intelligence permits. Other studies give material to think about, in these days a bewildering amount and variety of it; these basic studies enable one to *think about* the information. Slight the disciplines of word, number, form, and what results is a people given to accumulation of undigested data.

Some critics think that the current neglect of these disciplines of word, number, form, is due to the fact that they *are disciplines*. They involve a good deal that is not much fun for either teacher or pupil: drill, repetition, recitation, memory work. It is hard to engender a joyous attitude toward learning in terms of grammar, the multiplication table, exact measurement. Such basic tools of thought can be mastered only with such travail by both teachers and pupils as Americans find distasteful. As a people we are given to trying to make life as easy as possible for ourselves and for our young ones. We believe that "all work and no play makes Jack a dull boy," believe it so much that we forget that "all play and no work teaches pupils to shirk." The joy of learning often must be a postponed joy, the right to which is won by present drudgery. One can no more teach the art of thinking without such drudgery than one can teach without drudgery the art of playing the piano.

At any rate the critics are persuaded that the pupils are not being competently attended to in respect to word, number and form. If school people protest, and many of them do, that the reason they cannot teach these basic tools of thinking as well as schools used to teach them is because formerly the only ones who went to school were potentially competent to think, whereas now the schools must teach all the children, including the intelligently incapable, then the critics answer that at least those who can think ought to be taught how to use the tools of thinking and that this is just what is not being done. For the sake of the incompetent, the competent are penalized. That may sound like a democratic way to behave, but it results in fuzzy-minded inefficiency and confusion.

The second charge is that good manners are not being taught in the schools: a decent reticence, a lack of noisy self-assertiveness, respect for the rights of other people of whatever age, tolerance and consideration.

The modern schools seem under the false impression that children acquire good manners more or less by nature, that they are little adults almost from birth. This is simply not true. Each child is born a little savage who must be taught how to behave, at first under external coercion by his or her elders, then gradually, only gradually, by a growing appeal to reason. Never, in childhood, adolescence or adulthood, should one be permitted to behave as an anarch who rides roughshod over other people and expects to get away with it. This is what American children quite generally do. The schools frequently allow this immoral and antisocial attitude, sometimes encourage it. This negates a growth into constructive citizenship.

The third charge is that there is too little insistence in the schools upon achievement as the price of approval and promotion. Why should an able student work hard and use his brain if other students who are lazy or incompetent or both enjoy rewards equal to his own? The child is apt to see no sense in doing such a thing. There is engendered an easygoing attitude toward life and work, a feeling that the world owes one a living whether one bothers to earn it or not.

The fourth charge is that by permitting, by their silence almost forcing, pupils to ignore religion, the schools are turning

*out graduates who look on life in a fashion only three-dimen-
sional instead of four-dimensional. The fourth dimension is a
perception of reality deeper than that which sensory observation reveals.*

This assumption of a numinous fourth dimension has
been and still is the chief element in making man Man
instead of merely a canny and frustrated beast. Our schools
act as though this fourth dimension, if not nonexistent, is
negligible. This helps to impoverish the inner resources of
the American people.

The difficulty involved in reintroducing attention to
religion into the publicly supported schools is known to
the critics quite as well as to the criticized. How can religious motivations be imparted to growing boys and girls
who live in a country which is religiously heterogeneous?
What teaching in schools about things of the spirit can
possibly satisfy Catholics (Roman and Anglican), Evan-
gelical Protestants, Semi-humanist Protestants, Orthodox Jews, Reformed Jews, Secularists, Scientificists, Athe-
ists? There is no religious common denominator in the
United States.

Nor can an acceptable scheme be devised to teach "religion in general," striking out all things about which the
various religions differ and retaining that on which they
are agreed, which latter turns out to be only some general
ethical principles with no sanction behind them except

opportunism, alleged social advantage and the welfare of the omnipotent State. Some such vague and dubious scheme is about all that the public-school theorists so far have seemed able to think up in their occasional but increasing moments of concern with the problem of religion. Such an approach to religious teaching might satisfy the Secularist, the Atheist, the Humanist, even some who call themselves Jews or Christians but who deny the relevance of God; but such pabulum will never be regarded as genuinely sufficient by those who are affiliated with more definite varieties of religion. As H. H. Horne once put it, "To reduce religion to its lowest terms and to teach the residual as religion will satisfy no religious man and no religious communion."[1]

This is not the place to discuss all the perplexities involved in this problem and its possible solution. The literature on the matter is very large and exceedingly confused. Among the more helpful discussions of the matter are those by two educators, both Protestants but neither in any sense a party man. One is J. Paul Williams of Mt. Holyoke College, in *The New Education and Religion.*[2] The other is Frank E. Gaebelein, in *Christian Education in a Democracy,* the chapter on "Christian Education Looks at the Public School."[3] Some of the many discussions of this problem are rational but most of them are emotional and prejudiced.

My own advocated solution is much too simple to be at present palatable; but at any rate it does recognize facts. This is the argument:

1. A nation which does not give knowledge of religion to its children and encourage their commitment to religion in some form, is in grave moral danger. Its children, and later its adults, find no sanctions for ethical behavior except habit and expediency, and these are weak reeds on which to lean.

2. Religion cannot be taught merely as "another subject." To be effective, religion must permeate education in every subject; the school itself must be religious.

3. There are many religions in America, no one of which has a right to monopolize the schools or to appropriate all the funds provided by taxation for the schools. But in our present public school system, which has a professed desire to be fair to all faiths and to teach the peculiar tenets and practices of none, all religions *except one* are in practice negated, and to that one religion is given monopoly care. The religion of the public schools is a nontheistic and merely patriotic Secularism. The public schools, without its being generally perceived by those who direct the schools, have become, because of this monopoly advocacy, the most dangerous opponents of religious liberty visible on the American horizon.

4. Because of all this, if we desire the preservation of

real religious liberty in the schools, each major variety of religion in America (including of course Secularism and Atheism) must not only have the right but be encouraged to conduct its own schools *and to run them at public expense.* Such various schools must be and can be unified by rigorous public control *in all matters except religious teaching.* If we are not willing to have something like this multiple system, and certainly for the moment the American people is not, then let us stop talking about a competent religious education in this country and rest content to go on producing a secularist nation with a merely expediential morality.

I cannot see any flaw in this reasoning. If there is any, I should be obliged to have someone point it out to me. It will not do merely to protest against the remedy which I have advocated *unless the objectors offer something constructive in its stead, which in fact no one has done.* At any rate, the godlessness of our schools, not their antigodness but just their godlessness, is the chief problem to be considered in respect to those schools. The difficulty is real, vital, basic. It cannot properly be escaped; but it is being evaded by school people generally. As long as it is dodged, the contribution of American education to the production of moral character and citizenship will be, to say the least, somewhat limited.

The fifth charge is that the schools hold back boys and girls who have better than average brains and a desire to know and achieve. In the grip of a notion of "equality" contrary to demonstrated psychological fact, we endanger our way of life. (Was it not Lord Acton who said that if democracy dies it is always equality that kills it?) The idea is to treat all the pupils as though they were equally intelligent. The standard of achievement is set to fit the average, which is fair-to-middling low. The result is a mediocrity which frets and frustrates the more able while it flatters the incompetent. This mediocrity is making Americans increasingly a set of dull dogs, standardized in opinions, fearful of argument, clichéd in conversation.

Add these five faults together, say the critics, and the pupils will almost certainly come out incompetent to live intelligently and bravely in a democracy or to make contribution to social welfare or to resist unscrupulous propagandists or to get on to such adulthood as makes for increasing personal happiness through youth, through maturity to a serene old age. Add them together and one becomes properly alarmed for the future of our land. Those so mishandled will remain children, first spoiled children and then disappointed children.

The reader will please notice what these criticisms are and what they are not.

No mention is made in them of an assumed necessity for continuing the rigidity of an oldtime schoolroom. No one is faulted for insufficient application of the cane or the birch rod. No one is advocating that only "the classics" shall be taught. No one is worried because a study of this, that or the other discipline involved in facing a new body of proven fact is being substituted for consideration of those disciplines older and more conventional. No one is desiring to ignore the many improvements in teaching method which modern psychology has suggested. All these may be good or bad, right or wrong, without affecting the contention of these critics.

The faults they advance as being important, and deadly, are those which have been enumerated. The indictment means what it says and nothing more. It seems necessary to give this warning because when a similar analysis to this appeared lately in a general magazine, quite a number of pedagogic theorists denounced those of us who think as we do because, so they said, we deprecate many sorts of improvements in education which, as a matter of fact, we had not mentioned and which those of us who criticize admire quite as much as anybody else does. One was forced to conclude that there are at least some professors of education who cannot read.

All these five charges are vigorously denied by many but by no means all who control the schools, formulate the theories on which they are run, dictate to teachers what to do and how to do it. One sometimes wonders what sort of boys and girls many of the high-up pedagogic experts have met, so unlike are actual children to those whom the savants sit in their studies and think up and write about as typical and normal. Teachers, who must deal with real children, are not often taken in by all this curious theorizing. They know better, even when they are properly cautious about publicly disagreeing with the powers that be lest they be penalized for nonconformity.

What do most teachers think about the schools? It is not easy to find out. Next to nobody in authority asks their opinion, even though changes suggested by experts, real or alleged, who speak from schools of education, are valuable only if and when they have been tested and approved by the rank and file of those who do the actual teaching. These, in the last analysis, must determine which of many proposed changes will do more good than harm and which of them can be implemented with the money and personnel available. Few teachers are geniuses, but most of them are anything but fools.

All this being so, it is remarkable that no competent study of the opinions of the present-day American teacher has as yet been made carefully, comprehensively, in confidence. There is need and opportunity for some educational foundation to elicit and make available information about whether, in the opinion of teachers generally, the schools are doing or can do what is now expected of them;

and if not, what seems to them the value of various proposed improvements.

This need was lately brought home to me because I had the benefit of unsolicited opinions from a considerable number of teachers, some of them obscure and others anything but obscure. I realize anew how valuable teacher reactions can be. Over eight hundred of them, singly and on their own initiative, wrote to me about certain not too laudatory criticisms of public schools which I had uttered, first in three magazines of large circulation, then in a book.[4] Eight hundred is a small number among the over a million teachers in America; but what they had to say contains few surprises for those who have known many teachers privately, personally, informally; and if anyone thinks that the comments of the eight hundred are not typical, let him make a survey for himself, first making it plain to those surveyed that his investigation is confidential.

This last must be looked out for because most teachers are afraid to speak their minds, and this not without reason. One of my correspondents puts it thus—a teacher who, inquiry has revealed, is one of the best, by reputation anyway, in New York City:

"Most public school teachers must do and at least pretend to think what they are told by administrators, many of whom have had small teaching experience and who listen much too readily to professors of education who have, for the most part, had even less teaching experience than they. These administrators and their preceptors form a mutual admiration society of pontiffs of the pedagogic rite, with all prerogatives of the cult. For the teacher to initiate a thought or to express a hesitation wholly to believe whatever she is told is most unwelcome. Curiously enough, it is called 'undemocratic.' There is constant danger of reprisals, even of excommunication."

Another, who teaches in a Midwestern city, writes, "You may ask why I do not speak up about the schools as I have come to know them? Well, I have no desire to stick my neck out. Even the mildest overt criticism and I am likely to find myself transferred to some school which is next to inaccessible to my home. It is not only policemen who have been sent to the sticks."

These may be extreme statements; but it is not without significance that over three-fourths of my teacher correspondents are unwilling to be identified for fear of somebody or other. One marvels at the effective way in which "those higher up" have thrown dread born of insecurity into the hearts of most of the teachers, then have rammed down their unwilling throats revolutionary pedagogic doctrines and practices contrary to that humanology on which European-American civilization has been built during the long centuries; *that they have done this in the name of "de-*

mocracy in education"!

About four-fifths of the teachers agree that the criticisms leveled at the schools by those—and they are not few in number—who fault the system along the fivefold line mentioned a few pages back, are justified in so doing. But over two-thirds of them think that the blame for things being as they are is not to be ascribed wholly or even chiefly to the schools. They say that school people are helpless. They must do, can do, only what Americans want done with their children. Just as a country gets the government it desires and deserves, so with education. The low-grade stuff to which critics object, and rightly object, is what the misled community insists upon.

One of my correspondents, the principal of a large high school in a prosperous suburb, writes: "I am bound at every turn by the *mores* of our people. I try to do the best job I can according to my lights; but I have long learned that the family of a reformer has mighty slim eating."

Another principal, this time of a slum grammar school, writes: "I and my teachers know the faults of my school better than any outside critic can possibly know them. We do nothing to remedy the situation, nothing basic. We do not dare to try. To do it would bring down on our heads the wrath of the neighborhood and of the politicians who in the name of the public control our financial support. As long as our citizens do not know what an education is and cannot be made to understand it, we must just swallow our pride, sit on our conscience and be—what we are. We must do this or else leave the profession, which is the way out taken by thousands of American teachers every year." Again and again this note is struck. One wonders a bit if there can be much improvement of our cultural pattern through the schools if administrators and teachers are content to behave not as men and women but as mice.

Another thing which is stressed by many of the teachers who write me or with whom I talk is that in the education of youth formal schooling plays only a minor part; that this is particularly true in those phases of education which tend toward character development. Morals and manners, they say, can never be adequately taught in schools. They are caught from the community directly, extrascholastically: from family conversation, ideas, ideals and practices; from sensational newspapers, comic strips, cheap magazines, tawdry literature in general; from ubiquitous advertising on billboards and in a hundred other insistent media; from television programs and over the radio and from the movies; from dress and talk and common behavior as these reveal themselves everywhere.

From these sources, rather than from the schools, children derive their estimate of values. They are apt to get the idea that to be a real American means to share enthusiastically and uncritically in the sort of culture we were looking at in our first chapter. That culture is based largely on: (1) an overestimate of the value of possessions, comforts and amusements; (2) an aggrandizement of sensory appetite, particularly that of sex, out of all ratio to real importance; (3) a notion that the only way to judge the morality of word or act is by whether one can get away with it; (4) a conceit that to wisecrack is as effective as to be wise; and (5) a conviction that it is clever to get something for nothing, to obtain reward without labor. These are not the ethical bases on which America was built nor those on which any nation can long be maintained, but they are the impressions hammered home to children by life around them; and there is little the schools can do to correct them.

"Against the prevalent morality," writes a New York high school teacher of long experience, "the morality which is hedonistic, expediential, subhuman, the morality which is shouted at every child from birth, morning, noon and night, you and your kind seem to think the schools can effectually prevail. You are wrong. It cannot be done. I do not think it ought to be done. To try it would mean to endeavor to persuade our boys and girls that their parents, their friends, their cities, their country, are morally defective. Never in history has a people been rescued from basic immorality by schools persuading the children that their elders, and presumably betters, are bad actors. Social reformation does not begin in the schoolroom."

It is also evident from these letters that there is a general resentment against teachers being forced to attempt too impossibly much. Not all are as bitter about it as a junior high school instructor in Spoken English who must teach five sections of forty pupils each, two hundred in all, in sessions that last forty minutes each.

"A minute to a child," she moans, "in which to detect and correct physical and psychological speech defects, some of them serious, to overcome foreign accents and locutions, to acquire facility in making friends and influencing people and to become interesting and worth while through proper use of the spoken word. What's the use of trying? If I took my job seriously, I'd go mad."

This is an old complaint but it has gained new force in these days when teachers are more and more expected not only to teach academic subjects and to develop skills but to relate the children, while still children, to every problem of adult living. Let another teacher, this time in a Pacific Coast metropolis, speak for scores of others as vexed as she but not so eloquent.

"I wonder," she writes, "if those who criticize so severely the American teacher, contemporary model, and the school in which she teaches, know what the teacher's life has come to consist of. Each of us in this very modern school works, in the first place, forty hours a week in the building. My own immediate room charges number thirty-eight.

"What do we teach there? Scraps of literature and art, some unsystematic applied math, bits of history and geography—in fact, smatterings of almost all things, academic and otherwise. These we try to 'integrate around vital central interests,' such as how to date and mate and if possible avoid divorce; how to reform the City Hall and run the United Nations, how to plan cities, how to provide adequate housing, how to solve economic problems. All this when the pupils are 15 years old!

"We must teach the elements of reading and writing, too. The young ladies and gentlemen are supposed to have learned these down in grammar school, but few of them have fifth-grade facility, some even less. We have no fixed curriculum, which is a bother. We make our curriculum up from week to week, sometimes from day to day, trying always to entice 'pupil interest,' and we do it with 'pupil advice.' The students run the show; we are their patient servants, perhaps not always entirely patient when we discover that most of our young charges have been brought up with the ridiculous idea that inexperienced and ignorant children ought to be as much in control of education, and of life, as their informed and experienced elders.

"At four o'clock the day is over. But is it? There are still frequent staff conferences to attend for our indoctrination in progressive theory and practice. There is usually an hour or two of paper work, essays to correct, etc. There are 'projects' to set up. We must, moreover, assist in extracurricular student activities: chaperone picnics and dances, coach debating teams and dramatic clubs, that sort of thing. We must do our bit, in short, to amuse the young not only in school but after school too, so that they may be distracted from adolescent fornication, from smoking 'reefers,' from juvenile delinquency in general. Oh yes, we are supposed also to visit the homes of our pupils, to study their social backgrounds, and to act as personal advisers, helping all of them to 'find themselves as beginning adults.' Ours is the life of Reilly. Don't you agree? We labor more and more exhaustingly, and do nothing really well."

The comment just cited puts its finger on what is probably the chief weakness of the schools. Instead of being content to deal better and better with what was formerly their chief business, namely, trying to develop ability to think and to create, through specific academic disciplines, they now try to relate "the whole child" to "the whole of life." They desire, in other words, to combine the older functions of the school with the educative functions of the home, the Church, the family doctor, and any number of social agencies. The burden has become too great. Of these many functions none is being fulfilled competently. It may just conceivably be possible for an exceptional private school to do with a fair approach to proficiency all these various things, but this is not possible for the public school as at present staffed, equipped and financed.

To do what the public schools are being asked to do, depended on to do, would require, in the first place, a different and greatly more expensive physical equipment. It would require the erection of new buildings to replace the present ones, almost none of which has a proper working plant for "total education." It would require the doing away at once with overcrowding. To attempt progressive education with anywhere from thirty-five to fifty children in a class is absurd. A maximum of fifteen is the largest unit that can be contemplated if this newer type of thing is to be realized. National authorities point out that to carry on schoolwork even in the old-fashioned way we shall have to provide within the next decade 520,000 new classrooms. We should need, for the new type of education, at least 1,000,000 new rooms. Much longer school hours would also be necessary, practically the whole of the pupils' day and for six days a week, and this for the whole year round with no long holidays wherein the pupils are corrupted by parental controls. It would be necessary to provide scores of thousands of playgrounds, too, each under skilled supervision, and no end of well-equipped shops for creative activity. There would need to be facilities for health, for skilled physical and psychological adjustments. No end of things would be demanded without which "the relating of the whole child to the whole of life" is mostly gusty talk, talk which fools the public, talk the hearing of which makes more than a little ashamed of themselves the more honest members of the teaching profession.

The teaching force is also insufficient in numbers, and almost certainly must remain so, for the undertaking of such a job as is glibly advocated. The insufficiency is more apparent every year. The shortage of teachers is so alarming as to make it not too likely that we can carry on the schools much longer even on the present basis. This is no exaggeration. To replace teachers who die or resign and to provide more teachers for the instruction of the rapidly increasing child population—over a million additional pupils every autumn—we must find approximately 80,000 new teachers a year; but 32,000 is all that are being prepared for teaching and graduated annually from all the universities, general colleges and teachers' colleges in the United States put together. How are we going to meet this deficit of 48,000 teachers a year? Where are these new-type schools with vastly expanded functions, with necessity of one teacher to twenty pupils at most, instead of one teacher to forty or more, going to find man power and woman power? They would require at least 125,000 new teachers a year, or four times as many as we are now enlisting and training.

Nor is the present body of teachers intellectually equipped to carry on the proposed "total education." Of our 1,000,000 teachers, over 300,000 have been inadequately educated *even for their present limited tasks.* Nearly 100,000 American teachers in elementary schools have not even gone through a high school. This is one in ten of the total number. Of those who are rated "reasonably educated," very few have gained the psychological, sociological and methodological knowledge required for even a decent try at "total educating." It does not much help the insufficiently trained, either, to go off for an occasional summer session, a "refresher course," in some teachers' college where they get little more than a smattering of the patois of modern progressive theory. They return to their classes and try to practice the new pedagogy without having understood it. Nor does indoctrination by principals, supervisors and superintendents greatly assist the majority whose basic knowledge is inadequate, not even when the principals, supervisors and superintendents know what they are talking about, which is by no means always the case. To turn out preceptors who are able seriously to go in for what today is being stridently advocated and inexpertly practiced, would take at least seven years of study beyond the high school. There are few of the present staffs who have been so prepared, and few of those thinking of becoming teachers will tolerate the expense and long delay involved. Neither they nor the public authorities can afford it.

There is no getting around the fact that while our present teachers, and any we are likely to get, may be fairly competent to work in old-fashioned subject-matter-and-mind-training schools, they are simply not up to acting as preceptors, fathers and mothers, priests or rabbis or other ministers of religion, skilled counselors, trained nurses and psychiatrists, all these rolled into one. It is not honest, not intelligent, for professional theorists to talk as though this is not the case, thereby leading the general public to suppose that the public schools ought to do, are doing, what in fact they cannot do; encouraging teachers to neglect what they are able to do in order to dabble about in any number of tasks at which they are necessarily incompetent.[5]

Finally, the cost of the newer type of education, as has been shown by the experience of those experimental schools which have gone in for the whole thing seriously, cannot be less than triple per capita what the cost of the public schools is now. Will the American people stand for a 200 per cent increase in instructional costs? Could they afford it, especially in time of national and world emergency? Whatever may be the philosophical merits or demerits of "the new ideas," it would seem certain that they cannot be adopted unless they can be paid for. Otherwise, the result will be only more incompetence, further pretense, confusion worse confounded.

Are the schools, then, in a hopeless state? This does not follow. But it is significant that there is a widespread feeling, sometimes conscious and sometimes unconscious, among the rank and file of school people that they are caught in a trap; that they are being asked by the theorists who control school procedure to perform so many and such varied tasks that effectiveness in doing any of them is impossible. There are many things deplorable about the schools, but this is the chief of them. A cure is required if our education is to be rescued from befuddlement.

Those who staff the schools are admittedly in a bad way. They are notoriously underrecompensed, often paid less than the janitors, unrewarded by much popular esteem. They are run ragged by pupils who are the victims of exaggerated theories of free expression, whom they are forbidden to discipline, who are often out of control at home and everywhere else. They are patronizingly browbeaten by theorists many of whom, and these the most vocal, will not face facts or listen to reason. They are grossly

overworked in respect to hours and to the number of pupils each must handle.

All this is hard enough to bear, but when they are also
greeted by complaints that they are too lazy, too unwilling, to grasp the new pedagogy, and that this is what is
wrong with the schools, they are apt to feel that it is more
than they can take. Their first reaction is toward defense;
then, when no one heeds their plea, they are only too
likely to relax into frustration and cynicism. It is this,
quite as much as lack of pay, which causes so few young
people to consider teaching as a lifework, and it is a major
reason why thousands of teachers quit the profession every year.

The schools can be saved, but only popular insistence
on common sense can bring about the saving. As long as
the school authorities continue to be victims of an illusion
of omnicompetence, and as long as we the people dump
our children at the school door and say, "You are to take
charge of these boys and girls and relate the whole child
to the whole of life; and don't you try shoving responsibility for them back onto us; and mind you do all this
without increasing the school tax rate," just that long the
schools will continue to be what they have become. It is
said much too often these days that American school people
are falling down on the job. The truth is that the job,
ridiculously expanded in response to unrealistic theory

and consequent popular demand, has fallen down on them, and is crushing the life out of them.

American life in respect to manners, morals, character, ability to think clearly, has alarmingly deteriorated during the first half of the century. Our culture is becoming, indeed has largely become, the distressing sort of thing we were looking at in the first chapter of this book. Is the school sufficient to save us? Certainly not if the pedagogic "experts" who are in control are encouraged to continue to talk too big, while the schools in consequence perform too little. Certainly not so long as most of the people, the taxpayers, the parents, are satisfied with what is being done to and for and with the children.

III

The Church

The identification of religion with the particular cultural synthesis which has been achieved at a definite point of time and space by the action of historical forces is fatal to the universal character of religious truth. It is indeed a kind of idolatry—the substitution of an image made by man for the eternal transcendant reality.... Apart from the cultures which are idolatrous in the sense that they identify their own form with the divine image, there are still more which attribute to their way of life and their social tradition a universal moral or spiritual validity, so that in practice they are identified with the divine order and the moral law.

—CHRISTOPHER DAWSON

IN THE FIRST CHAPTER OF THIS BOOK I SUGGESTED that we take a good straight look at what the pattern of living has become in mid-twentieth-century America, at why our way of life is in danger of debacle, at how it is increasingly difficult for anyone with sensitivity to human possibilities to live in such a civilization as ours simply, honestly, bravely, satisfyingly. I arrived at a conclusion, in which I hope a good many of my readers share, that our present difficulties are so great and so basic as to demand nothing short of revolution, not so much political revolution or economic revolution as moral revolution, a revolution in estimate and pursuit of values.

In the second chapter, I maintained that we must take a view of education realistic enough to bring recognition of the limitations of our schools to initiate and carry through the revolution required, to promote any sort of ethical attitude which does other than reflect the current patterns of behavior, twisted and dangerous though these are. I made a statement, the truth of which is attested to one who looks about him by the evidence available, that whatever else our public education may do for society, it is little likely to put common living in America on the human bases necessary for long survival of our country. One must extend this attribution of incapacity for ethical education from the school to the home, for the home is also an educational institution, a more important one than the school in developing character. The home has come to function so badly that the schools have felt they must try to assume parental responsibilities. School and home have become so stereotyped, so conformist, so complacently secularistic, that they are not merely incapable of resisting and correcting a growing corruption but have actually become proponents of that which leads us toward catastrophe. Their guilt, though few recognize it, is great.

Let us now turn our attention to organized religion, to the Church as a possible mover toward revolt against an essentially subhuman scheme of living; to ask how and why the Church fails us in the emergency which we begin to know must be faced and dealt with; to inquire what can be done, if anything, to restore the Church to the performance of that task which is its reason for being, the task of confronting mundane cultures with eternal morality, confronting a failing world with God.

When one recalls how great has been the impact of the Church upon society in the past; when one sees, for instance, the former impact of the Hebrew religion upon the cultural life of those who professed that religion; when one remembers the formative influence of the Christian fellowship, its ideas and ideals, on human affairs in Europe or in America up to say fifty or sixty years ago; it is surprising how small a part the Church has come nowadays to play in changing or preserving the current way of life. It is even more strange to observe how few Churchmen, cleric or laic, seem to recognize that in our time such small respect is paid to religious standards of value that most of the younger generation do not even know what those standards are. It is most odd of all to notice how few even of those Christians who say they are for Christ and of Christ seem much to regret the general relegation of religion to an individualistic, pietistic, merely cultic level.

There are, it is true, still a great many of us who are at least nominally religious adherents. According to the Yearbook of the National Council of Churches there are, roughly speaking, 87,500,000 Americans who say they are affiliated with some sort of religious body. This does not mean that all of them, or even most of them, are greatly interested. So far as a forming or reforming of culture goes, there might as well be, perhaps might much better be, fewer of them and those more concerned. Their average giving for the support of religion, for instance, is laughably less than their average expenditure for movies or cosmetics or tobacco, or sweets and chewing gum, not to mention television sets. Their contribution runs to less than twenty-five cents a week per person. More important, surveys have shown that only about one-third of alleged Christian Church members, Catholic or Protestant, on any given Sunday bother by worship to honor God and affirm fellowship in God's adventure. As for Jews, a very much smaller fraction than one-third bothers to attend public worship. Most of them go only at the high festivals, and this more as a racial affirmation than as an act of devotion of Yahweh. Nor can we be too sure even of the alleged membership statistics as given in the Yearbook. Anyone who knows much about the lists kept by local congregations is aware that almost all such rosters are padded. Rarely is anyone removed from the rolls unless he or she is known to be dead, and not always then. A member may have shown no interest for years on end; he may be unknown to the pastor or to anyone in the congregation; still his name sometimes stays on the list. In a certain city one communion made an honest self-census in 1951 which showed that while that district reported to its national headquarters a membership of over 60,000, less than 38,000 could after the most diligent search be found. This sort of exaggeration is common. But let us admit, albeit skeptically, that there are 87,500,000 Americans who are associated with some religious body or other.

The thing that needs asking is what the religion of these 87,500,000 counts for in forming the pattern of American life. The necessary answer is, "Very little indeed." Many ecclesiastics seem to suppose otherwise. One wonders sometimes whether they really think that what they say about the Church's present cultural potency is true, or if they are whistling to keep their courage up. Probably a mixture of the two. Certainly no competent sociologist or political scientist, no scholarly observer of our country who is not himself a professionally ecclesiastical person, says or thinks that the Church has much to do with the complexion of the contemporary American picture. Instead, their usual conclusion is that most Americans regard the Church as promotor of a respectable minor art, charming if it happens to appeal to you, *its only moral function to bless whatever the multitude at the moment regards as the American way of life.* The Church may be relied on to advocate certain incidental improvements in the cultural pattern, though rarely does it initiate any of them. It co-operates, rather, with secular good works. The Church certainly is not generally expected critically to examine into what our way of life is like, much less to go about resisting it.

There is small expectancy, then, that those who belong to the Church will be able to set this reeling civilization of ours right side up and then steady it. The Church and its people too largely conform, unconscious that they do conform, uncritically conform, almost automatically conform, to the compulsions of current culture. They seem largely to have forgotten that witness to a divine moral law in the face of a worldly secularist human society which has always constituted, and still constitutes, religion's right to claim social pertinence. The world, hurtling on toward political, economic, psychic catastrophe, is not going to be saved, if it is saved at all, by the Church if the Church remains an uncommitted host of politely respectable people, willing to be led by professional ecclesiastics whose methods of promotion and administration are just about as worldly as those of the sick society they say they wish to reform but which, as a matter of fact, deforms them almost as easily as it deforms everybody else. If the Church is to help in restoring the world to moral sanity, there must first be revolt and recovery of moral sanity within the Church.

The Church has need to stop regarding itself as an end to be served and to resume acting as an instrument for God to use in the rescue of human beings from worldliness, from self-centered incapacity. For Christians, this means for *God as He is in Christ* thus to use it.

Christians today are too much given to trying to take refuge in the Church lest they have to face the Christ-God. If one may borrow a figure of speech from Kierkegaard—he used it in another connection—the Church is too largely being prudentially employed by its adherents much as a small boy, fearful of being spanked by the schoolmaster, puts a napkin in the seat of his britches so that the impact may be less uncomfortable. Or, to change the comparison, most Christians today appear to seek a sort of vaccination against Christianity, with a solution of one part Christianity to nine parts respectability, racial inheritance, ecclesiastical regularity, good-fellowship and geniality. The grace of God is so diluted by this inoculation as to make Christianity powerless to excite or disturb. The same thing is true, *mutatis mutandis,* of the Jews.

To the extent that this has happened, the Church has become to most of its adherents a substitute for God. A deadly substitution it turns out to be, both for humanity, which needs redemption and finds it not, and for the Church itself, which is more and more regarded by people generally with indifference or even with the kind of amused contempt expressed by T. S. Eliot in "The Hippopotamus."[1] In this poem Mr. Eliot is not scorning the Church as God intends it to be, His mystical and revolutionary Body, made up of those committed to the task of moral resistance to the world and redemption of the world, but only the Church which has been corrupted by the world, has forgotten its Lord, has made God into an idol to be patronized, not a Deity to be feared and obeyed. This is the sort of Church which "sleeps and feeds at once," which is "wrapped in the old miasmal mist."

Organized religion in contemporary America, Catholic

and Protestant and Jewish, tends to exalt, admire and enrich itself. This is why it is so much less dynamic than one would suppose from observing its statistical reports. Will it cease so to be conformed to the collapsing world and be transformed, and itself become transforming, by the renewing of its mind?

There is too much of what Annette describes in a letter. Annette is a musician, an actress, gay and brilliant and good and decent and happily not too conscious of it. She knows the world. She found the reality of God a few years ago, and happiness and courage. She married and moved to a city which may be left nameless and to a Church which we can call St. Wilfrid's. "This parish," she writes, "has everything, from an exquisite and mostly unused chapel to a great and noisy community house in which the young riot about and their elders have smokers and tea parties. It is all impressively active; but is it religious? Its people love it, boast about it. It makes me slightly sick."

We all know too many such parishes. Sometimes the gilt is a bit tarnished, the atmosphere a little musty; but those who belong are fond of it, gaudy or dingy, much more than they are of God. In such places, and they are legion, God is "kept in His place," revered in theory but neither adored nor obeyed. In them His utterances do not sound clearly enough to disturb the status quo. The vulgarity of the Gospel is covered by the sonority of Latin, or romanticized by Hebrew emotionally charged, or semi-concealed by the quaint charm of King James English. The sermons are interesting enough to keep the congregations awake but not uncomfortably probing. The benevolences go to remedial rather than reformative charities. The result is the sort of pseudo-piety vigorously described some years ago by Vida Scudder of Wellesley College: "A Church pleasant-voiced; endangering nothing in particular; an ornament of the Sunday pew; devoted to good causes in proportion to their remoteness; ignorant alike of the ardors of the mystic or the heroisms of the reformer; cheerfully assured that whatever is innocently agreeable is religious; a domestic religion, calculated to make life pleasant in the family circle; curiously at ease in Zion." The impression is somehow given that the function of the Church is partly to further whatever is desired by the parishioners, partly to be patriotic without discrimination, partly to provide a living for ecclesiastics. It is as though God were being regarded as a sort of handyman at the service of nice people. If the Church is again to become significant in these days of crisis, it must escape from such impious self-absorption.

If this is to happen, the Church needs to regain consciousness of the all-demanding majesty of God. This age has lost a sense of obligation to that which is beyond humanity and beneath the physical. So has the Church. This loss is the chief of many things the matter with our culture, principal cause of the blindness which makes contemporary man seek happiness and inner peace, without finding them, in terms of materiality. We seek "all this" but not Heaven, not even "Heaven too." A Church which would help restore sanity to our time must free itself from preoccupation with materiality; it must rediscover, vividly and possessedly, a vision of the reality of that which is more than material.

For such a rediscovery a sound and unambiguous set of theological convictions about man and about God is required, convictions sufficiently tested by time to be undisturbed by transitory changes, by such things as war or class uprisings or new fashions in either gadgets or philosophy. Such clear-cut convictions are not easily noticeable today in American religious circles.

There is, rather, a babble of theological contradictions. Even the man in the pew or at the altar is apt to be none too clear about basic matters involved in the faith to which he is more or less attached. As for the man in the street, he is bewildered and put off by an apparent inability to agree, not only about nonessentials but about the thing that matters most, about who and what is the God who is offered, about that for which the God is offered, about what is the nature of God's relationship to man. It is hard for John Doe, to whom it may occur that just possibly religion may have some light to throw on present confusions, social and individual, to discover, from the allegedly religious sermons and pronouncements which he hears or reads, just which of two very different theologies is being commended to him. The uncertainty in his mind is not caused, as is often supposed, by competing denominations. The ambiguity crosses denominational lines; it would be found in any pan-denominational Church unified on lines other than theological. The variance is not about such small matters as the nature of Biblical inspiration or forms of ceremonial or modes of ecclesiastical government. The variance goes much deeper.

On the one hand there is that kind of belief which Christianity held when it converted Europe, when in the past it vastly influenced social patterns, when it made the saints. It is the religion not only of Catholics but also of historic Protestants. It is as much the religion of Luther, Wesley, William Temple, Tillich, Niebuhr as it is the religion of Athanasius, Anselm, Teresa, Maritain, Fulton Sheen. Those who believe this faith of the ages and try to live in accordance with it are controverted by what may be termed "neo-Christians." These used to call themselves "Modernists" but now prefer the term "Liberals." They may, and frequently do, retain some of the older forms of Christian devotion and sometimes, though not often, recite the older creeds; but when they employ these they put into them meanings radically different from those which these creeds and forms of worship have carried for nearly two thousand years. The two groups differ in what they teach about God. Their basic variants have immense cultural implications, for they involve contradictory notions of the nature and destiny of man, and therefore of society.

The Christianity of the centuries has always held, and still holds, that natural man, man apart from God, is an unreliable creature except for this: that one can count on his getting nowhere that satisfies him in individual living, and on his inevitably ruining, by war or other mad device, the social fabric which he dreams of and tries to realize. This continued failure is not primarily due to man's ignorance of technology or of social psychology; it springs from a deeper defect. Man leaves undone what he well knows he should do, does what he is aware he must not do. He is, to use the conventional language of Christianity, a being sin-possessed. Education will not necessarily help man, not enough. It may easily make man more dangerous than otherwise he would be, more effectively an iconoclast and a killer, more potently mad. Increase of creature comforts will not solve man's problem. It may, and frequently does, make man lazy, vain, greedy, quarrelsome, superficial; it may result only in his more speedy self-ruin. Because the folks are what inherently they are, man gets nowhere much by way of progress in time; he tears down what his fathers built and builds what his children will reduce to rubble. His tale is a mixture of developments and decays. He gazes into the future for meaning instead of trying to search for meaning for the present in the light of the past. He rides on a merry-go-round which takes him over and over again to where he was before. This, of course, is what the Bible teaches about man. It is also what the study of history reveals.

Since there is no salvation for man by way of what is called "progress," historic Christianity maintains that man can be rescued from futility only by the intervention of God, of a power not of ourselves that makes for righteousness. Human beings, so historic Christianity insists, can be saved from themselves and lifted out of the tragic round of self-seeking failure by laying hold on the hand of the Infinite, that He may lift them from what they are into something of what they were meant to be, wish to be, themselves cannot become. Historic Christianity, in short, is a religion of redemption, of divine rescue for man from an otherwise inevitable inanity. Participation in this redemption, historic Christianity goes on to say, is made possible for man by God working within His Church, a body of believers who are incorporated into God's very being in Baptism. They can then be fed by the imparted comradeship of Christ the God-Man, guided and made strong by the Holy Spirit. To those who are convinced of man's fatal flaw and God's intervention, which means 99 per cent of the Christians of the past and very much the greater part of Christians today, religion has urgency, since they are sure that without God, without redemption, without grace, nothing faces the individual or society but a senseless whirligig the true name of which is Hell.

Until lately no Christian, whatever his minor differences from his brethren, would have denied all this. This is the faith which sent the martyrs happily to death, inspired the confessors, made the holy ones. It is the faith of Augustine of Hippo, Francis of Assisi, Dante, Thomas Aquinas, Newman, Christopher Dawson, Dorothy Day. It is equally the faith of Hus, Shakespeare, John Donne, Milton, Wesley, Wilberforce, T. S. Eliot, General Booth. It has been and is the faith of millions of people, including many of the highest intelligence and scientific proficiency, as well as of more simple people the reality of whose spiritual achievement demands respect.

There has grown up also a quite different sort of Christianity. Its adherents are sure that man is by nature good and that he will get sufficiently better if only education is made more generally available and environment improved. To them Jesus is not God come to save man from himself. They see no need for such redemption. To them Jesus is a moral teacher and a good man, no more. He is the son of God only as we all are God's children; He differs from us in degree of divinity but not in kind of divinity. To them prayer is a process of affirmation of the highest values that they know, but is not otherwise effective since there can be no possible intervention from that which is beyond or behind the sensible universe. God is the Good, the True, the Beautiful; in Jesus one sees the Good, the True, the Beautiful portrayed in great loveliness. He is to be honored, His sacrificial life imitated if possible; but after all He is only human and dead and neither to be adored nor besought for aid. The ancient creeds may be said if one desires, but only as poetry. The sacraments are only dramatic devices by which we remind ourselves of the example of Jesus and of the love and kindness of a God who is imminent but not transcendent. As for the Church, it is a voluntary association of earnest people who wish to help one another become more like Jesus the man. This is Liberal Christianity.

It is impossible to maintain that these two Christianities, which compete for popular interest and following, are varieties of the same religion. They are incompatible in essential belief about man, about society, about God. If one of them is true, the other is not. In both camps are good people, sacrificing people, honest people. But is man capable of getting better and better by his own natural development or is he doomed to perpetual failure unless God intervenes? It makes a deal of difference which of these alternatives is correct, a difference not merely in theoretical doctrine but also in one's attitude toward living, one's source of hope and happiness, in social action too.[2]

The advocates of the second sort of Christianity are a small minority of Christians, but their opinions receive notice all out of proportion to their numbers. This is natural enough, for their teachings are what the public for the most part has desired to hear. They have reflected and magnified the exaggerated optimism about man which has become characteristic of us, which is the chief cause of our decay. Liberal Christianity has been especially popular in America, where humanistic optimism has been more prevalent than anywhere else in the world except perhaps in Russia. Insofar as there is now growing a new skepticism about the possibility of man's lifting himself into Heaven-on-earth by pulling on his own individual or collective bootstraps, Liberal Christianity sounds more and more unreal. There is strong revolt against it even in what have been some of its strongest centers. A sick and sorry humanity, when it does turn to religion for possible help, is less and less interested in spiritual doctors who keep praising the very thing that causes the sickness and pain and bid the patients indulge in more of the same.

The influence of the Liberals is definitely on the wane; but they serve to confuse the populace. It is thanks to them that it has become hard for John Doe to get at what Christianity actually teaches and at what are the social and cultural possibilities of Christianity when understood.

The point I am getting at here is that as long as the Church's spokesmen speak sometimes in terms of one of these Christianities and sometimes in terms of the other and sometimes in terms of an unthoughtout mixture of the two, it is hard to see how the Church can give effective help in the solution of our cultural problems. It does make a difference whether or not those who offer God as an answer to man's need make plain what they think man is and what they believe God can contribute and does contribute toward man's assistance. As long as the Church's spokesmen seem not clear about these basic matters, there will be less and less use looking to it for help in clarifying cultural muddles.

Secondly, if a Church is to be vital enough to influence morals and manners, its adherents must not only think clearly and speak with reasonable unanimity about man and about God; they must adore God. Something more than formal adherence to forms of doctrine is required; this something is moral commitment to that which is deemed unshakable certainty. This is particularly necessary in times of popular perplexity about everything and everybody. A religion whose followers are unwilling to try heroically to live, if necessary to die, rather than deny One whom they adore, is not worth much as a religion, not from any point of view.

Commitment is both strengthened and made plain by worship; but such worship as involves commitment is almost a lost art in England and America of the twentieth century. In Catholic circles Christian worship has tended to become formal and mechanical; among non-Catholics, vague, of doubtful pertinence, often just plain tiresome.

The word used for "I worship" in the New Testament means literally "I kiss the hand" of a leader and master, do it in reverence and loyalty. If the Church is again to stand firmly and effectively for its view of life, it needs to relearn how to kiss the hand of God, how to put vastly more emphasis in its worship upon Him who is being worshiped than upon the people who are engaged in worship. After the Reformation the Mass and the Divine Office, the God-centered simplicity of both of which had characterized the Christian cult for fifteen hundred years, were gradually discarded by Protestants and a man-centered worship, often an individualistic man-centered worship, more and more took their place. For many decades, indeed, a sense of God's supreme otherness, His majesty and holiness, to some extent remained; but gradually, under the influence of the pantheistic introspection which is characteristic of humanistic Liberalism, Protestants have largely lost a genuine realization of the presence for worship of a God greater than any man or than all men, yet a God sufficiently self-revealed in human terms for people to understand Him and to love Him, a God to be humbly revered and implored. Among American Protestants worship has become more and more denatured; more and more a matter of human affirmation.[3]

To the extent that the Church has ceased to adore God, to that extent the Church no longer brings with persuasive authority to bewildered and confused man a sure sense of Christian commitment. The Church has too much come to resemble a social club plus a forum for the exchange of human wisdoms. There are already plenty of clubs and forums without the Church turning itself into another one. A Church with God at the periphery of worship and life seems a superfluous institution.

There are many in the Church who understand the necessity of its reorientation toward God. They see that it has fallen into disrepute because it has ceased to be religious enough. They are trying valiantly to do something about this; but it must be admitted that the results of their reforming zeal are not yet too visible. American Protestants still continue for the greater part to go in for mutual self-cultivation rather than attempt to get, by adoration, beyond man to God and then, having found Him, to go forth to obey Him. Meanwhile American Catholics, both Roman and Anglican, have tended to let their worship become too polite and perfunctory. To the extent they have done this they have failed to use their greatest appeal to the religiously searching.

With confusion in Christian circles themselves about what man is and God is, and with watering down of worship of the Christ-God, the Church imparts little certainty about the moral implications of following such a God, nor courage of conviction. The moral teaching given by Christ Himself, that social wisdom which the Church is supposed to offer to a decadent culture, is so simple that the modern secularist American has doubts of its sufficiency. He is sure that if a thing is true it must be hard to understand. As Chesterton once put it, "The way is all so very plain that we may lose the way."[4]

It takes no unusual gift of brains to perceive what Christian morals are. The difficulty is not intellectual but volitional. What is required, says Jesus, is that we shall love God utterly and that because we love Him in this fashion we shall love, also in this fashion, every man, woman, child and chiefly those, our neighbors, with whom our contacts are immediate and inevitable. This sounds like a platitude until one asks what it means to love.

To love means to place another at the center of one's life. Do I love my child? I do if my child matters to me more than I matter to myself, if I regard myself as existing to make it possible for the child to come to a true maturity. If this is lacking in me, if what I chiefly desire is that my child shall amuse and serve me or, even worse, that my child shall not bother me, shall not prevent my doing as I please when I please, then I do not love my child; I love only myself. Do I love my friend? I do if I am willing to be to that friend a servant of that friend's sustenance, looking on that friend with thought not of what that friend may do for me but of what I may do for that friend. Do I love my wife or husband? Only on terms of self-investment does even conjugality release me from that enslavement to myself which is the chief cause of human woe, the parent of damnation.

My beloved, my parent, my child, my friend, my mate, may or may not love me in return, or may once have loved me in return but have ceased to love me in return. That does not fatally matter. If he or she does not love me in return, I still can love. "If you love only them that love you, what profit is that to anyone?" asks Jesus. "I say to you, Love even them that are your enemies, them that reject you, treat you with contempt. So shall you become the children of the Eternal Father."

Without such loving, says Jesus, there is no hope for society.

Without the loving which makes no demand on love,

as some of us who work for God in universities know only too well and keep on insisting, education is apt to produce knowledge without wisdom, to implement evil as well as good, to augment cupidity, to render men the more dangerous to one another.

Unless we learn to love without demand of love, war, that monster whom we have equipped with claws of unbelievable deadliness, is a perpetual inevitability. Without such loving, a pawn nation like Korea is fought over until in one year three million of its people, most of them noncombatants—the old, mothers and expectant mothers, babies and little children—innocent of offense except that they live in that unhappy land, are "liquidated," as the current phrase puts it, while 70 per cent of all Korean buildings—homes, factories, schools, hospitals, temples to the gods—are obliterated. So it will be, or worse, in every land, including ours, when modern war is waged therein. Without such love as makes no demand on love, man's long career on earth approaches an inglorious end.

Loving without demand of love, Jesus insists, is no impractical sentimentality, not a matter for pretty speech in pulpit or elsewhere. Far from it. Loving without demand of love is the only means to prevent disaster to our country, damnation for the human race. We must love or we shall die, hopeless, frustrated, defeated.

The scheme of behavior taught by Christ is an elaboration of the command to love in this manner. For this sort of loving, socially indispensable but extremely difficult, Christ promises divine assistance. He reveals in Himself that God is a perfect lover. Men and women, all of whom are incompetent lovers, afraid to love, when they approach the Christ-God in prayer and sacrament can be touched by Him, empowered to dare the impossibly necessary. God comes into the world that He and His may love the world into effective joy. Though the world knows Him not, yet He keeps on loving. He comes to His own and even they receive Him not; they reject Him over and over again. Yet He keeps on loving. Finally, God's persistent love can break down man's unloving cowardice. God can make His own the sons of God, free to care utterly, free to suffer vicariously for the unloving, co-redeemers with Him of a sick humanity. This is the authentic wisdom of Christ. To it the Church in our time gives only muted witness, scarcely more than verbal assent.

Not long ago I lunched in Boston with a youngish man, able, earnest, honest, distressed. He said, "The world is damned, as you say, by self-seeking, pride and greed; but so, it seems to me, is the Church. The world has bought the Church up, put it in bondage, is taking it along to Hell." "It does look that way, perhaps," I replied; "but this means only that the Church must again be watered by that which can restore new life to it." "You mean," he said, "by the lives of confessors and the blood of martyrs. Well, I think I could believe in the Church if I saw its people declare their independence of the world and suffer deeply and without complaint because they had done it. I suppose there are some who do, but mighty few. Lots of people are as skeptical as I am of seeing any significant resistance by Churchmen to the *mores*. Church leaders once in a while speak out, sometimes quite clearly, but the Church as a whole pays no attention. The Pope thunders out truth about society, for instance, in the encyclical 'Quadragesimo Anno'; but the local fathers do not teach that encyclical. They seem to be too busy hoeing their ecclesiastical potato patches, whipping up parochial activities, accumulating property, augmenting income, playing politics. It is the same with Protestantism. The World Council of Churches occasionally issues true prophecy; but in the local congregations the preaching is of milk and honey, and the practice too."

Though I, who am a Christian and a Churchman, see the dead-aliveness of those (my brethren and myself) who constitute today on earth what God intends to be the militant Body of Christ, for all I cry aloud for sackcloth of repentance, for a covering of the head with ashes and a begging the Lord for pardon, yet I do believe that the Church will survive, that in cultural importance and influence it will revive. I cannot forget how time after time in the past God has raised the Church out of impotence as great as that which it manifests today, has rescued it from cowardice and compromise, has sent it forth to save men from the ruin they have wrought. But equally I have not forgotten the cost of such restoration: confiscation, persecution, death of the body. These the faithful have not refused. I am confident that the Church's children will again accept the fire without flinching and come out purged. I do not hide nor would I have others hide from the fact that the Church at the moment is conceited, cowardly, sycophantic, of the world as much as in it. Until that is admitted by Christians, and paid for, the Church will be not hated but ignored.

As over and over again in the past, God the Holy Ghost must come, will come, to His Church, lighting with flame as of fire, fire that burns, painful but purifying. He will come like a rushing, mighty wind, filling all the house. God send that day, and soon! But meanwhile, can man in his distress expect to get much help from the Church toward America's cultural regeneration?

As long as Christians are contented to conform to America as it has become, as long as by observing their conduct domestic, business, political, it is impossible for the man in the street to tell who is a Christian and who is a pagan, the Church will be regarded by thoughtful people, and quite properly, as hypocritical or else as sentimental, emotional, ignorant alike of the tragedy of man and of the reality of its professed religion. Just that long the Church will remain culturally insignificant. The gentleman in Boston was bitter, but he was right. Eventually the Church will be saved from being what it is, saved through those who take religion seriously. Until that happens it seems downright foolish to expect that the Church will be of much help in saving our culture from debacle.

IV

The Rebels

A democracy in which everybody had an equal responsibility in everything would be oppressive for the conscientious and licentious for the rest.

—T. S. ELIOT

THE AMERICAN WAY OF LIFE SEEMS LARGELY, dangerously, to involve two false assumptions.

The first of these assumptions is that the Common Man, who today in our country has been emancipated politically and to a large extent economically, who has learned how with astonishing facility to make and manage machines and to distribute the products thereof, can be trusted also, without skilled critical leadership, safely to run himself and society. This Common Man, usually well intentioned and well heeled, has not in fact learned how to handle his new freedom and his new wealth with expertness, with suavity. He usually has small understanding, nor does he as yet desire much more of it, about what constitutes the good life, the sort of life that gives significance and happiness to man as man, to man as more than the beasts. A reasonably mature approach to human problems seems mostly beyond him. He has much curious and useful knowledge but very little wisdom.

The Common Man in America is encouraged, by those who would be lifted to power on his shoulders, to think and act in ways dangerously provincial. He may or may not remain a political isolationist, but he certainly appears to be a cultural isolationist. The American Common Man is largely cut off from respectful contact with those who live in other lands, other continents, other civilizations. He is persuaded, and rightly, that we have tremendous things to teach to other peoples, but he is not aware how much we may learn from them. This deprives us of correctives which we need. It is not conducive to world peace, either.

There is another type of isolationism, even more dangerous, which prevails in America. We separate ourselves not only from the rest of the contemporary world but also from the past. We neglect the store of humane wisdom painfully acquired down the millennia by experimenting man. We are conceitedly, absurdly, of the opinion that almost everything worth man's knowing about himself and his society has been discovered only recently. We and our children look to the physical and biological sciences, the high development of which is indeed modern, to reveal all man needs to know, ignoring the fact that these sciences tell us about man only as an animal. We disregard the humanities, the liberal studies which are as old as the race, the learning about man as more than beast, the learning which must be mastered if human beings are to be free and responsible.

A survey of one hundred representative universities, reported by Benjamin Fine,[1] showed that in the two years 1950-52 there were drastic cuts in the number of professors in the United States who were employed to teach the humanities. This was due to a rapidly decreasing number of students willing to study such subjects. There was no corresponding drop in the number of those required to teach the sciences. "College authorities report that while they can retain all their chemistry, physics and applied science professors, they must reduce the rolls of their full-time professors of English, foreign languages, the humanities generally. The fields of foreign language, history and English seem to be the hardest hit.... Moreover, the survey indicates that the colleges and universities expect in 1952-53 to have 19% fewer students in the humanities, social studies and liberal arts than they have today." The same decline in interest in the humane studies is even more plainly visible in surveys made of the development of curricula in American secondary schools. This decline has been going on with increasing rapidity for the last twenty-five years. Because as a nation we have less and less training in humane studies, we are more and more conformed to a pattern of thought and action less and less stable or humanly satisfying. We are shockingly ignorant of what, in the light of man's history, constitutes a healthy human pattern.

About this the Common Man needs guidance, such guidance as can come only from those who know things about humanity, past and present, which the multitude does not know, does not at the moment see much need to know. If the ancient, tested, civilizing wisdoms are to be preserved until that day when the American Common Man rediscovers his want of them, specially trained individuals are required who are prepared to swim against the tide.

This brings us to the second of the two false assumptions on which Americans today are trying to build a way of life that will prove sound and safe and satisfactory.

It was supposed by those who founded the United States, even as it was supposed by those who developed European-American civilization down the centuries, that social groups exist for the safety and proper development of the individuals who make them up. The individual, or so our fathers thought, needs to be protected from the tyranny of the group quite as much as, maybe more than, the group needs protection from individuals on the loose. But of late we act more and more as though social groups have essential existence apart from and superior to those who are their constituent members; that to do the group will is the inevitable and sufficient business of each one of us. We Americans recognize that this is a mistaken idea when we see it in alien totalitarian regimes, and loudly we deplore it. We fail to notice the extent to which we too have committed ourselves to the collectivist heresy, the extent to which deviation from mass standards is gladly tolerated only in matters which are deemed of no importance. It is not surprising that the Common Man does not perceive this tendency when even Dr. James B. Conant, the President of Harvard University, insists that private schools are an evil because they prevent uniform devotion of pupils to a directable uniformity throughout the nation.[2]

This placing of the crowd ahead of the individuals that make it up would have seemed to Marx or Lenin an indication of our sound development. It could not help but gratify the late John Dewey also, to whose disciples we have almost wholly entrusted the direction of American public education. The assumption back of Mr. Dewey's pedagogics is that the good life consists in following group desire. To the Deweyites a sound education is one which accustoms the pupils to discover group convictions and then conform to them. This is known as "becoming socially adjusted." By an act of faith, certainly not on the basis of evidence past or present, they assume that group desire is certain to be *good* desire, that the group is always more trustworthy and wise than anyone within it. The idea of critical and corrective leadership by exceptionally equipped people is regarded as anachronistic. It smacks of "indoctrination," whereas both knowledge and righteousness emerge through "group dynamics." In other words, no one may rightly judge Demos except Demos. God, insofar as there is one, is synonymous with Community.

Happy is that person, that people, which has discovered this and acts accordingly. Happy, and of course safe, our America will be if only we continue, under the direction of relativists, to look on the critical individual who feels sure that in this or that important respect the community is at a given moment mistaken, as an enemy of the people, to be sent to Coventry or to some place even harder to endure. By obeying majorities freedom is insured, freedom to conform.

Somehow or other, though, things are not working out too well in the relativistic sort of democratic society beloved by Mr. Dewey and his disciples. The group seems to be going sour. There is more and more to deplore in our civic life, our industrial life, our business life, our family life. The theory of a self-sufficient and wholly contemporaneous democracy, subject to no criticism except its own, if judged by its works would seem to be romantic, out of touch with reality. The facts belie the theory. The results become increasingly intolerable, rapidly so intolerable as to endanger the continuance of democracy altogether, so intolerable that once again the Common Man may soon be clamoring for the Man On Horseback. God forbid! But it has happened that way over and over again in history. It has happened that way in our own time in various great countries that once were democratic.

Against totalitarianism, which is the antithesis of democracy, against Fascism or against Communism (they are basically the same) or against some native American brand of the black beast, what can prevail? Not the short-sighted, morally indifferent sort of democracy which our way of life engenders and fosters. Not a democracy which looks on society as a proper field for enterprise so free that instead of serving the common good it seeks greedily to exploit the same for personal or class or chauvinist advantage. Not a democracy which seeks to do as it pleases, which ignores what is both God's law and the truth discovered in the long past about various ways of human behavior and their consequences. Not a democracy which forgets the primacy of man's spiritual aspirations or the reality of his spiritual responsibilities. Only a democracy that serves more than Demos has ever long survived, can survive.

This nation is composed of Common Men, a wonderful lot but for the most part ill-informed about how and for what man must live if he would be happy; untrained in how to live together so that togetherness may conduce to mutual welfare. That these things may not be forgotten or, if forgotten, that they may be relearned, there is need for sane, constructive, fearless critics who will not conform to pattern merely because it is pattern.

Our nation needs skilled diagnosticians, well versed in the history of man and ready to examine contemporary behavior patterns in the light of what that history reveals. They must be wise enough to realize that our ancestors were not all fools and that the long view is more likely to be correct than the short view. They must be perceptive of the ways in which man is beast and acts like one, but equally perceptive of the ways in which he is more than beast and acts accordingly. They will use the scientific method but not be obfuscated by scientificism. They must be aware that the voice of the majority has not always, or indeed very often, been the voice of God and that it cannot be regarded as necessarily that voice today. They must love all men but be unimpressed by multitudinous clamor. They must be ready to speak the truth regardless of consequences, even when not invited to do so.

We need such nonconformists if democracy is not to become absurd. No society can remain sane or safe without respectful consideration of what this sort of person says, without training of such people in schools and universities. We are not getting them. In lack of them lies great peril.

It may be objected that what is here being advocated is an elite. The charge is true, but not of importance. The elite suggested is a different sort of elite from that which was in control before the era of mass emancipation. That was an elite predominantly composed of a few who led because of accident of birth or by virtue of possessing unusual wealth. The masses, except for a few occasional geniuses who broke through into the classes and were reluctantly received by the classes, lived by proxy as it were, through the few who alone were civilized. Such a state of affairs will not be again, and ought not to be.

This does not mean, however, that every kind of elite is dispensable.

A democratic elite would consist of men and women who hold membership within it because, and only because, they have a trained intelligence which enables them to observe and understand man as man; because they are skilled in humane studies; because they are fitted to guide the Common Man into a life more and more sane and rich and satisfying. Such persons must be encouraged to emerge from the masses; and as they emerge society must pay for their special education. In a democratic society an elite can justify itself if, and only if, it helps the Common Man to perceive what the good life is, what the democratic life may become. By such an elite the Common Man can be assisted, though with difficulty, to become more than a well-paid hewer of wood and drawer of water and tender of machines, more than a mere producer and consumer of goods, more than an ant in a mechanized and collectivized anthill; helped to acquire the virtues of old-time gentlemen and ladies but without condescension toward anybody, much less contempt.

The Common Man, at least in America, has largely freed himself and his children from poverty and oppression and the fear of them. He is now beginning to perceive, dimly as yet, that such freedoms are not enough. Time was, to use Ortega's comparison,[3] when the many slaved away below stairs while the few enjoyed civilized living in the drawing room. The masses have now broken through from the cellar and taken possession of the whole house. This is to the good; but possession of the drawing room is not of great value, is often embarrassing, to the Common Man unless he has learned how to use the drawing room, unless he knows the amenities. The elite in predemocratic days had something more than material advantage, something which the masses, through no fault of their own, then lacked, and still lack. It is not enough to pull down the older elite from their former seats unless those of the democratic order can learn how to occupy those seats easily and effectively. No society of men and women, Common or Preferred, can live for long on bread alone or even cake, on gadgets and gewgaws, no matter how widely dispersed these are.

The masses need an elite, a democratic elite, an elite emerging from the people and held responsible by the masses to lead into a more urbane and humane way of living. The masses will not submit anymore to coercion; but they are beginning to get a little tired of being flattered expensively, enticed to get nowhere worth getting to, misled by a precious crew of low fellows of the baser sort who treat the Common Man and his children more cynically than ever they were treated by the formerly priviledged few, with a contempt the harder to endure because the newer bosses slap the Common Man friendly on the back before they rob him of his dignity. The Common Man is slowly but surely waking up to the fact that statecraft, economic sanity, sound thinking, cultural adornments, are not automatically the by-products of larger wages and less work, pleasant to have as both those things are. If life in America is to become as rich for the masses as it used to be for the privileged classes, expert guidance is required. Some sort of elite is inevitable. Why not develop one from among the Common Man's more gifted sons and daughters and educate it for cultural leadership? Why not through such a democratic elite impart to the people at large at least enough wisdom to perceive when and wherein the alleged good intentions of our current leadership, political and cultural, are phoney?

There is no use dodging the fact, though, that as yet Demos only faintly perceives the necessity for leadership by a democratically selected and liberally educated elite. Demos, it is true, stirs restlessly in a sleep induced by the heady fumes of a too speedy material enrichment and a too easy political emancipation. He has incipient nightmares; but he is not yet ready to awake and act. It will be a long time before he will know what is happening to him, a long time before he will tolerate, certainly not welcome, guidance from those who specialize in the understanding of human nature and experience. Demos does not yet appreciate the necessity of leadership from those who have learned to understand the good life and can help their fellows to see through the plausible shams which at the moment confuse American aspirants for happiness and significance; leadership from those who can explain to Americans their faltering civilization and their blundering selves.

Until the day dawns when a democratic elite will be welcomed and listened to in this country, the American who would himself escape from slavery to crowd culture must expect to have a difficult time of it. He may become a free man, but he will have to purchase his liberty at a great price.

There are those who are sure that the wisdom of ages past is something of which they cannot endure to be deprived. They are not selfish in this, not seeking refuge in an ivory tower. They are persuaded that they must help preserve for the Common Man a largely forgotten racial wisdom. They wish to help preserve it through a less than human present and a precarious future, perhaps through a period of debacle, into a happier day. They understand that both the making of their souls and also their most real service to our country depend upon their finding deliverance for themselves from pursuit of such obvious and ostentatious trivialities as satisfy the masses at the moment. Their most immediate problem is not how they may attain leadership but rather how they may accomplish and maintain their own release from crowd compulsions. They are sure that until they themselves are free they can neither know self-respect nor serve America's children and her children's children. The first thing to be said about that problem is this, that until the possibly distant day when the American Common Man has become disillusioned about the essential rightness of all he thinks and does, anyone who would escape from slavery to the mob and to the present exploiters of the multitude must expect to have a challengingly difficult time of it.

He must not mind being regarded as somewhat lunatic. He must count on being poor. He must look for small applause and few promotions, even when he tries to work in terms of supposedly idealistic institutions like a university or the Church. Harder still to bear, he must count on seeing his family ill-supported and vexed by him. Woe be to his wife if she be not devoted to improvident ideals and purposes to the same degree as is her husband. He must, in short, be an ascetic, moved by much the same sort of impulse, and willingly embracing much the same sort of discipline, as are known to him who forsakes the secular world for the cloister. Sometimes, indeed, the aspirant to freedom finds that he must literally go into a cloister; hundreds of Americans do it every year, including some very brilliant people indeed. More are called to take a different path than that, perhaps a more difficult path; but the requirement in any case is for great and cheerful austerity.

He who would prepare himself to withstand the crowd and so to become free should see to it that he gets just as good a liberal education as he can. This is not always gained in formal schools. Remember Abraham Lincoln. His schooling was rudimentary; he taught himself, and he made a good job of it largely because he knew the kind of understanding he was after and then with labor pursued the getting of it. Good schools can be a great help; poor ones can injure, often beyond remedy. This applies not only to lower schools but to universities. Academic degrees are not significant unless one knows in what fields they were taken, in what spirit the study was directed, for what end it was undertaken and brought to completion. The discipline required for the Ph.D. degree, for instance, is usually valuable as discipline; but discipline alone, within some narrow field, does not insure competence for living. It is required that one's studies give basic attention to the humane fields.

The aspirant who knows what is involved in human behavior will not be content merely to specialize in a science, valuable though that science may be. One can be a first-rate scientist and still not be much of a man. One must study science-plus if one is to become fit to help direct a culture intelligently or even oneself to participate in a culture. It is unfortunate for human welfare that so much university emphasis is laid today on scientific studies, particularly on those which have to do with applied science. It would help if every candidate for a scientific degree were required, as is reported to be the case at Cambridge University, to take work in the fine arts, in philosophy and in religion during his last year of residence and pass a competent examination in that sort of knowledge.

What more than science is to be studied by him who seeks cultural adultness? The answer to this question is that all should be studied which concerns man *qua* man. History certainly, lots of it, the record not merely of man's economic and governmental arrangements and disarrangements but of man's groping attempts to find meaning, his striving to maintain self-respect, his endeavor to live with other men in mutual joy despite continual disillusionments, his frequent near-despairs, his grounds for hope. To this end the aspirant will look at the writings of the great philosophers. He will read the best in literature, and ponder it. Especially he will soak himself in poetry, for in poetry more is revealed about the nature of man than in any but most extraordinary prose. He will examine not only letters but the other arts—music, painting, sculpture, costume, the drama, the dance—seeking not so much to become an expert performer or an expert critic as to discover what is revealed by human attempts at significant creativeness. He will make observations, too, of customs and manners, those of various places and times, particularly those of that tradition of which he and his neighbors are heirs. These disclose what man is in his intimate interpersonal relationships. The study of man's failures will engender humility and compassion. Consideration of man's occasional successes will reveal the price which must be paid to become and remain adequately a husband or wife, a parent, a friend, a lover, a citizen, a human being.

Yes, and man's religion must also carefully and sympathetically be taken into account. Men and women with rare exceptions, and all children, try to live, each according to his or her light, as servants of supersensible purpose. Religion cannot be ignored. Discredit mature religions and old and often vicious superstitions take their place. It is impossible to know what human beings are, and their cultures past or present, without knowledge of what religion is and does. The aspirant to understanding will make no such mistake. He will realize that to understand religion is a necessity if he is to become capable of gaining humane wisdom.

In this respect more, perhaps, than in any other he will find himself out of touch with the educational theory of his country. By carefully ignoring religion our public schools and colleges have made most of our citizens ignorant of the spiritual hungers of mankind and how to feed them. It has malformed what once was a profoundly religious country into one that is predominantly secularist, opportunist, amoral. It has turned out a nation with few considered goals, whose members no longer see themselves in focus. Our people are without an adequate sense of history, they have few convictions of purpose, next to no philosophical interest. They exhibit little ethical responsibility. It is because of these lacks that we are incapable of creating and sustaining a consistent foreign policy, that our domestic policy is largely one of competitive greeds, that our culture is frivolous.

A quite different sort of education from that ordinarily available is required for him who would help in the regeneration of our culture, an education summed up in the sayings of two wise men of an older day: "Nothing human is alien to me," and "The proper study of mankind is man."

The kind of education just suggested is useful not only for persons of top-notch mentality, for those capable

of profiting by university residence, for those fit to belong to a democratic elite. At least the elements of humane knowledge can be grasped, and will gladly be grasped,
not only by the erudite but also by the rank and file of
simple people, even by quite young children, if they are
exposed to the contemplation of human greatness. One
of the grave defects of current American pedagogy is its
unwillingness to impart to growing boys and girls an appreciation of the long, rich past. Such an appreciation
would help them, help all of us, to learn how to get on
with one another, by teaching us to get on with our elders
and betters, with our ancestors. It does broaden and mature to admire and imitate greatness, humaneness, when-
ever and wherever we come across it.

Children especially need this; they enjoy it, too. To
deprive them of it is to cheat and impoverish them. It is
also to endanger society, for the health of which not only
humane leaders are required but also humane followers.
To arouse respect and love for the great ones of the past is
the best way to contend against the pressure of mass con-
formities, whether the contention be carried out in houses
of higher learning, or in such gathering places of the Common Man as clubs and lodges and union meetings, or in
shops and factories and other places where people labor
together, or in formal schools for growing boys and girls,
or in homes. The great ones of the race have been invari-

ably and contagiously men and women who did their own thinking, who respected tradition and reinterpreted it and built upon the past. It is this kind of men and women that our generation lacks.

And if it is not tiresome reiteration, let it be said again and again that for discovery of tradition, for competent interchange of ideas, for the rehumanizing of the Common Man and the restoration of his dignity, for the salvation of America from crowd conformity, for the advancement of the liberating humanities, it is necessary that our people be taught *when young* how to read and write and speak and listen with competence, with due regard for words and what they mean. Without this basic skill, training in which is skimped today, no one can effectively explore the past, or the present for that matter. We must also be taught *when young* how to think logically—by mathematics is the easiest way to do it—so that the relationship of facts and ideas may be grasped with a minimum of wishful thinking, with the least possible deception, either self-deception or deception at the hands of demagogic mountebanks.

He who to any considerable extent has begun to escape the deteriorating pressures of crowd culture must exhibit great and sincere compassion. Otherwise he will find himself looking with a wicked distaste upon his less fortunate brethren. He will find himself echoing one of the most gracious but pitiless of American social analysts in our time, Albert Jay Nock. He used to say of the floundering Common Man, "He is a failure and a fool. The mob must be manipulated. Alexander Hamilton was right when he called it 'that brute beast.' The mob must be managed, and always will be managed, by the clever, the shrewd, the strong. The mob must be beaten, in the fashion of Hitler and Stalin, or else it must be bribed and flattered, which is the American way. The Common Man is Caliban, a clod."

Indeed Mr. Nock and that brilliant architect-philosopher, Ralph Adams Cram—they were great friends—seriously maintained that only a few, perhaps a tenth, of the allegedly human bipeds walking about are really, psychically human. The great majority, they thought, are subhuman, "Missing Links." The majority must be cared for, they pointed out, not for its own worth but only because by a curious freak of nature parents who are Missing Links can give birth, and sometimes do, to children who are psychically of the species Homo sapiens. The Missing Links must be so managed that they will be prevented from destroying civilization, which is and can be created and sustained only by the human minority. Those who hold to this opinion can, it must be admitted, make out a plausible case for it—but not a good enough one by any means.[4]

When this or anything like it is the attitude of him who has escaped crowd coercions, the Common Man will hate his inwards, and rightly so. It ignores the fact that the Common Man is not the only man that can fail. Caliban has been defective, but so has Prospero. Between the two there may be a gulf of difference in intellectual achievement, in taste, in manners; but both Prospero and Caliban are men. Because they are that, there are possibilities of growth in human stature for Caliban and Caliban's children. Equally, Prospero's learning, his sound philosophy, his mastery of the amenities, may push him the quicker and more surely into Hell by the road of arrogance. Prospero corrupted by conceit can loose more woe, can more corrupt our culture, can more effectively destroy our country, than a multitude of Calibans. Worse than the crowd is he who forgets the common flesh of which all men are made. This stultifying danger must be avoided. He who has been freed from crowd domination, he who has learned how to live a truly human sort of life, which is an art as yet for the most part hidden from the eyes of the many, must get that straight. The humanist in a subhumanist culture, the religious man in a secularist society, must never forget the divine law of *noblesse oblige*. In the brotherhood the strong must love and serve the welfare of the weak; the informed must love and serve the welfare of the ignorant; the wise must love and serve the welfare of the foolish; the righteous must love and serve the welfare of the wicked; those who are freed must love and serve the welfare of those still enslaved.

What is wrong with the Common Man? He is not wicked above other men. The trouble with him is two-fold. First, he has not learned to see life in all its possible richness. Secondly, he has lost contact with that which is greater than himself, from which (or Whom) he might gain courage to escape the crowd. He can be shown, but only by one who understands and therefore forgives. The greatest of all Common Men came from Heaven and from a carpenter's bench to teach humanity the perennial morality, how to live and how to die. It was Jesus the Christ, whom all mankind reveres and whom many millions adore, who said with a sublime compassion about those who impaled him on a cross, and thereby sealed their own condemnation, "Father, forgive them, for *they know not what they do.*" Any man who is himself enlightened with the wisdom of the ages and who desires to help others to a like enlightenment must have this same sort of charity, born of humility. The constant prayer of such a would-be benefactor must be, "From pride, vainglory and hypocrisy, good Lord, deliver me."

What have I been trying to say in these four chapters? *First,* that American culture is a crowd culture, provincial in its contemporaneity, dangerously trivial. *Sec-*

ondly, that far from our public education being able to rescue us from what we are, it has itself become the servant of our defective culture, reflecting our modern mistakes and with fervor encouraging our children to repeat those mistakes. *Thirdly,* that organized religion, to which one might think we could look for help in saving us from what we are, is too much organizational and not enough religious for the task. It seeks too avidly its own preservation, at cost of compromise. It seems afraid to tell the truth about God or man. Perhaps it is not too sure of what the truth may be. Its worship tends to be pedestrian, and its morality is far too much a sentimentalized worldliness. But *fourthly,* that we can be saved; our culture can be humanized and human dignity restored; our education can be rescued from those who now emasculate it; the Church can become once more truth-centered, God-centered. All this can happen—but only if we raise up rebels willing to pay the price which rebels always must expect to pay.

Does this age wish a recovery of sanity? Will the Common Man at last desire to learn how to make good use of his newly found political and economic opportunities? Will he, soon enough to avoid catastrophe, seek to participate in the richness of tradition newly grasped, tradition reinterpreted? Or will he continue to be led about and exploited by almost any plausible rogue? If the latter is true of him, our democracy is doomed! I do not know the answer to these questions. Many of us still have hope. Our faith in the potentialities of the Common Man is still as great as is our fear and detestation of the blather of the crowd. Against the latter we must be rebels, not because we hate the Common Man but because we love him deeply. This is our reasonable service, our religious duty.

Notes

CHAPTER I: THE CULTURAL PICTURE

1. These figures are from an article by Arthur Krock in *The New York Times, Feb. 21, 1952.*

2. According to a report to the Board of Education by Charles J. Bensley, chairman of the Board's committee on buildings and sites.

CHAPTER II: THE SCHOOL

1. In his *Psychological Principles of Education* (New York: The Macmillan Co., 1906), p. 386.

2. New York: Association Press, 1945.

3. One waits with hope and expectation for the publication of the report of a "Committee on Religion and Education" of the American Council of Education, a report due in 1953. This Committee, the director of which is Clarence Linton, Professor of Education in Columbia University, has been at work for several years on "an inquiry into the function of the public schools, in their own right and on their own initiative, in assisting youth to have an intelligent understanding of the historical and contemporary role of religion in human affairs." This searching study is being financed by the

Rockefeller Foundation. Over 8,000 educational and religious leaders, including Roman Catholics, Jews and every sort of Protestants, have been consulted. The forthcoming report should largely remove emotionalism from discussion of this vital matter. At least it is hoped that this will be the case.

4. Bernard Iddings Bell, *Crisis in Education* (New York: McGraw-Hill Book Co., 1949).

5. The figures used in the last few paragraphs have been furnished partly by the National Education Association and partly by the Federal Security Agency, Office of Education; the conclusions reached are my own and, I hope, those of my readers.

CHAPTER III: THE CHURCH

1. *Collected Poems* (New York: Harcourt, Brace & Co., 1936), pp. 49–50.

2. Those who sympathetically know about Judaism are aware that the same cleavage is found in that religion today.

3. "The average Protestant service hovers in atmosphere between a Kiwanis get-together and a Chatauqua lecture—both admirable things in themselves but not distinctively Christian. The barrenness of Protestant worship has reached such a point that many potential Christians are stopped short in their inquiries after one visit. They see in the service no values that they could not get from an adult education lecture, and they reasonably conclude that it is absurb and a little insincere to dress up an essentially secular event with the faded poetry of a Christian vocabulary." (*Room for Im-*

provement: Next Steps for Protestants, edited by David Wesley Soper. Chicago: Wilcox and Follett, 1951. The article on worship is by Chad Walsh.)

4. "The Wise Men" in *Poems of G. K. Chesterton* (New York: John Lane Co., 1915), p. 61.

CHAPTER IV: THE REBELS

1. In *The New York Times,* March 9, 1952, p. 1.

2. In a widely publicized address delivered in Boston on April 8, 1952, before many public school educators at a meeting of the American Association of School Administrators. Dr. Conant frequently indicates his sympathy with a hyperpatriotic regimentation of American thinking such as sounds suspiciously totalitarian.

3. In *The Revolt of the Masses.*

4. Albert Jay Nock, *Memoirs of a Superfluous Man* (New York: Harper & Brothers, 1943), p. 136 *et. seq.*

Index

express and deepen
conviction, 88–90; need
for moral reformation of
and in, 94–96; reflected in
theology of God and of
man, 80–88; as a refuge
from moral conflict, 75–
78; reported and actual
membership, 73–74
Civil Rights Act, xxx
Classics. *See* Western
literary tradition
Collectivism. *See* totalitarianism
Columbia University, x, 36
Comfort: harmfulness of its
overemphasis, 30; worship
of, xiv–xv, 28
Commager, Henry Steele,
36–37
Committee on Religion and
Education of American
Council of Education,
123n. 3 (47)
Common Man (current
American variety): comic
strips the fiction of, 14;
confuses wealth and
virtue, xii–xiv, xxxii, 26–

27; lacks critical leadership
skills, 99–110; man-
ipulated by the press,
14; seeks money and
recognition, xiii–xiv;
undiscriminating reader,
16–19; worships comfort,
xiv–xv, 28. *See also* new-
rich, Demos.
Conant, James B., 103, 125n.
2 (103)
Conformity: falsely viewed as
a democratic virtue, 7–8,
28; harmfulness of its
overemphasis, 29–31;
literacy and mathematics
as antidotes to, 117;
penalties facing teachers
for nonconformity, 52, 54–
56; of schools and homes,
72
Conrad, Joseph, xxxiv
Contemporary worship, xxiii,
88–90
Cram, Ralph Adams, 118
Crisis in Education (Bell), viii,
124n. 4 (53)
Crowd Culture (Bell), xi–xii,
xxxvi; Eliot's review of, xii

amusement, 20; as a poor
influence on character
development, 56
Music: as a cultural index, 12;
as a passive amusement,
19–20; as a proper subject
for study, xxix, 114;
wrongly indulging man's
sexual appetite, 27–28

*New Education and Religion,
The* (Williams), 47
New Historicists, xxviii
New-rich: its confusion
between wealth and
virtue, xii–xiii, 26–27, 57;
its cult of personality, xiii;
its overvaluation of
possessions, xiii, 26–27,
57
Newspapers: as a cultural
index, 12–15; as a poor
influence on character
development, 56
Niebuhr, Reinhold, 81
Nock, Albert J., viii, 118

Ohio Wesleyan University,
xxxix

Old-rich, xiii, 27
Ortega y Gasset, José, xv,
108
Orthodox Christianity, 81–84
Orthodoxy (Chesterton), ix
Overcrowded schools, 61

Papal social encyclicals, 94
Parents: condescending to
children, xxiv; overlooking
the importance of religious
training, xxiv; part of the
problem, 61, 67
Parochial schools, 47–49, 103
Part of the problem: parents,
56–57
Periodicals: contents dictated
by profit motive, 15–16;
as a cultural index, 12,
15–16; as a poor influence
on character development,
56; wrongly indulging
man's sexual appetite, 27–
28
Plato: on happiness and well-
being, xxxviii; his radical
egalitarianism, xxiv
Poetry: creeds as, 85;
unpopularity of, 17; value